Key Terms for Language Teachers

Key Terms for Language Teachers
A Pocket Guide

Alessandro Benati

SHEFFIELD UK   BRISTOL CT

Published by Equinox Publishing Ltd.

UK   Office 415, The Workstation, 15 Paternoster Row, Sheffield,
      South Yorkshire S1 2BX
USA   ISD, 70 Enterprise Drive, Bristol, CT 06010

www.equinoxpub.com

First published 2022

British Library Cataloguing-in-Publication Data

A catalogue record for this book is available from the British Library.

ISBN-13   978 1 78179 880 5   (hardback)
           978 1 78179 881 2   (paperback)
           978 1 78179 882 9   (ePDF)
           978 1 80050 166 9   (ePub)

Library of Congress Cataloging-in-Publication Data

Names: Benati, Alessandro G., author.
Title: Key terms for language teachers : a pocket guide / Alessandro
   Benati.
Description: Sheffield, South Yorkshire ; Bristol, CT : Equinox Publishing
   Ltd., 2022. | Includes bibliographical references. | Summary: "The main
   purpose of this Pocket Guide is to ensure that a clear and accurate
   definition of key terms and aspects of language learning and teaching is
   provided to the reader"-- Provided by publisher.
Identifiers: LCCN 2021039289 (print) | LCCN 2021039290 (ebook) | ISBN
   9781781798805 (hardback) | ISBN 9781781798812 (paperback) | ISBN
   9781781798829 (pdf) | ISBN 9781800501669 (epub)
Subjects: LCSH: Language and languages--Study and teaching--Terminology. |
   Language and languages--Study and teaching--Miscellanea.
Classification: LCC P51 .B419 2022 (print) | LCC P51 (ebook) | DDC
   418.0071--dc23
LC record available at https://lccn.loc.gov/2021039289
LC ebook record available at https://lccn.loc.gov/2021039290

Typeset by Sparks – www.sparkspublishing.com

Contents

Acknowledgements   viii

About the Author   ix

About this Book   xi

Introduction   1

 1   Age   13

 2   Communication   19

 3   Corrective Feedback   29

 4   Explicit and Implicit   39

 5   Focus on Form   43

 6   Input   53

 7   Instruction   65

 8   Interaction and Negotiation of Meaning   69

 9   Language   77

10   Language Tasks   93

11   Language Tests   117

12   Language Teaching Method   123

13   Learning and Acquisition   131

14   L1 And L2 Acquisition   137

15   Motivation   145

16   Output   149

17   The Role of the Instructor and the Learner   155

18   Working Memory   161

Epilogue   165

Bibliography   171

Acknowledgements

I would like to thank my students and colleagues for their valuable feedback. My special gratitude goes to the anonymous reviewers who have provided me with priceless advice on how to improve the content of this book. I would also like to express my appreciation to everyone at Equinox, and to Janet and Valerie for their continuous support during my career as language teacher and scholar. A special thank you to the University of Hong Kong and, in particular, The Louis Cha Fund for their support in this project. Finally, I would like to thank professor Víctor Parra-Guinaldo for his contribution to two of the entries of this pocket guide book.

About the Author

Alessandro Benati is the Director of CAES at the University of Hong Kong. He has previously worked in the United Kingdom at the University of Greenwich, University of London, Middlesex University, University of Portsmouth and at AUS in the Middle East. He is internationally known for his research in second language acquisition and second language teaching. He has published ground-breaking research on the pedagogical framework called Processing Instruction. Alessandro's research reflects his long-term commitment to making theory and research accessible to non-specialists. He has delivered both nationally and internationally several teacher training programs to help improve teaching practices and policies. Alessandro has coordinated high-impact research projects funded by the EU, Leverhulme Trust, British Academy and other research bodies. He is co-editor of a new series for Cambridge University Press called *Elements in Second Language Acquisition*, a member of the AHRC Peer Review College and the REF Panel 2021. His collaborative and interdisciplinary research make use of new technology (e.g. eye tracking, computational modeling) to track what happens within language learners' brains in real teaching/ acquisition contexts.

Contributor

Víctor Parra-Guinaldo obtained both his Master's and PhD in Rhetoric-Composition, Linguistics and Applied Linguistics at Arizona State University and has since taught a variety of composition and linguistics courses at the undergraduate level and for the MATESOL program. His research agenda lies in two main areas: historical linguistics, and in particular morpho-syntactic phenomena within the Germanic and Romance language families; and applied linguistics, including second-language teaching and learning and pedagogical practices. He has published his latest research with Routledge and Springer, among others, whereas his first publication was a book of poetry at the age of 23. Dr Parra-Guinaldo is a member of the Linguist List International Linguistics Community, the Linguistics Society of America (LSA), and the Society for Germanic Linguistics.

About this Book

The main purpose of this *Pocket Guide* is to ensure that a clear and accurate definition of key terms and aspects of language learning and teaching is provided to the reader. Curriculum and language teaching materials must be genuinely informed by what we know about the nature and role of language and language acquisition.

This *Pocket Guide* peels back the complexity of some of the key terms and aspects in language learning and teaching to reveal some basic notions that readers should know about.

Key features of this guide are:

- Easy, reader-friendly style with no citations
- Jargon avoided where possible and technical terms explained in context
- Summaries of main points provided
- Suggestions for additional readings.

Fifteen main entries are chosen for the *Pocket Guide*. Each entry is easily readable and accessible to specialist and non-specialist readers. It is written avoiding a scholarly style and tone using a reader-friendly approach. Key readings are provided at the end of each entry.

Each entry contains the following features:

- Can we take a minute to think about this?
- What is the nature and role of …?
- What are the main points?
- What else can we read?

Introduction

One of the key objects of inquiry for language scientists is the concept of language viewed as a mental construct and representation. Language teachers often work in the dark, with little understanding of the object of their efforts and often lacking a clear understanding of the role and nature of language and language acquisition.

What is language?

Language is a complex, abstract, and implicit system which consists of the interaction of several processes and mechanisms in the mind/brain of the learner. It is complex because learning a language means acquiring a number of its elements (e.g. the total stock of words, the sounds that make up words, the patterns of word formation, the rule of sentence structure and so on). Language is composed of abstract principles which bear no resemblance to rules found in language textbooks and are difficult to describe with exact words. This complex and abstract system is also implicit as we know we have language in our heads, but we don't really know what the contents are. This implicit system is a vast network of forms and lexical items which grows in our head as we process more language and make form-meaning connections. A network of forms and lexical items are linked to each other via semantic relationships (e.g. sad and funny); formal relationships (e.g. interesting and interested); lexical relationships (e.g. interesting and interest); and syntax (e.g. Subject–Verb–Object) that governs sentence structure which informs language learners of what it is possible and what it is not possible in a target language. There is an important distinction to make between language as a complex, abstract, and implicit system and language as a skill. Skill is the ability to use language in real time and it involves the intersection of accuracy (produce error-free language) and fluency (speed in using the target language). Language learners acquire skills by participating in skill-based activities. Language is special as it is not learned in the same way as other complex mental phenomena. Humans are hardwired to learn language and have special cognitive mechanisms specifically designed to deal with language.

To what are first and second language acquisition the same thing?

There are some similarities and some differences between the acquisition of a first language (L1) and a second language (L2). Both L1 and L2 learners need input to construct a language system. However, children normally master their first language with relative ease, whereas adults attempting to learn a second language struggle to achieve this. Quantitative and qualitative differences in input are one of the reasons which explain possible disparities in L1 and L2 acquisition. There are similarities in the way L1 and L2 learners acquire morphemes (a morpheme is a small unit of language which carries a meaning. Simple words such as car, house, ball are morphemes. If we had an -s- to any of these words we have two morphemes: the root word car and the plural marker -s-. Each of these two morphemes carries its own meaning: one vs. more than one car). L1 learners follow a sequence of acquisition for a number of function words in English as an L1 (e.g. nouns, verb inflections, articles). Similarly, L2 learners acquire grammatical features of a target language in a certain order and this is regardless of their first language or the context in which they acquired them (progressive -ing is acquired before regular past tense -ed, which is acquired before third-person -s). A further similarity is the acquisition of certain language marked and unmarked features. Unmarked features are those that are universal or are present in most languages and which learners tend to transfer. Marked features are language-specific features which the learner resists transferring. Unmarked features are learned earlier and easier than marked rules in both the L1 and the L2, while unmarked forms require more time and effort by the learner.

Children have an innate and internal ability to acquire the grammar which is not influenced by external factors. Adults, on the other hand, no longer have this ability, and resort to use problem-solving skills to learn a language. Children are usually considered to be better learners than adults. They tend to have fewer inhibitions than adults and have a desire to actively participate in the social life around them that helps them to learn new languages. They do not have analytical skills and tend to process languages generally through sensory experience, and language develops from exposure to simplified and concrete input. The difference in context of L1 and L2 acquisition plays an important role in the acquisition process. While it is possible to learn an L2 in various contexts, L1 acquisition takes place only in a natural context and in the social group in which the child is grow-ing up and where the child gets L1 input only.

What is the role of transfer?

The role of transfer is still very much debated in second language acqui-sition. However, it must be noted that L1 transfer cannot be attributed to acquisition stages or order of acquisition. L2 learners seem to go through predictable and specific orders of acquisition of morphemes despite their L1s. In relation to errors, they are not simply a result of L1 interference as there are other linguistics and cognitive processes that explain why L2 learners make errors. Very oftern language instructors wrongly interpret errors as a form of transfer. L2 learners (L1 = English) often produce ut-terances in the second language (L2 = French) that resemble L1 sentences such as *Je suis vingt ans* (instead of J'ai vingt ans, meaning = I am twenty). This type of error is not transfer, but a communicative strategy of dressing up an L1 utterance in L2 vocabulary,

What role does input play in language acquisition?

Input refers to the language that language learners are exposed to and has a communicative intent. Language learners hear or read the language that contains certain linguistic features (e.g. vocabulary, grammar, pronuncia-tion, etc.) and other information about the language. These features make their way into the learner's language system only if they are linked to some kind of meaning and are comprehensible. Language learners acquire lan-guage mainly through exposure to comprehensible and meaningful input, in a similar fashion to how they acquire their first language. The input that language learners receive should be simplified with the use of contextual and additional meaningful clues. Simplified input consists of a variety of characteristics: slower speech rate (and thus clearer articulation), use of high-frequency vocabulary, pausing at appropriate places with pauses often longer and more frequent, rephrasing, and the use of shorter and simpler sentences. The use of shorter sentences, for example, reduces the informa-tion-processing burden on the language learner. Additional pausing does the same thing: pauses give learners 'processing time' before the next round of information comes in. These modifications result in a greater likelihood of comprehension, which in turn facilitates the conditions for acquisition.

Input, to be effective and useful for language learners, must have two main characteristics: (i) it must be comprehensible, and (ii) it must have a communicative intent. Features of language make their way to the system if they have been linked to real-world meaning. However, it is not possible for language learners to take in all the input they are exposed to as humans have limited capacity to process and store information.

Conversational interaction and negotiation can facilitate acquisition. Negotiation for meaning, and especially negotiation work that triggers interaction adjustments by the native speakers, facilitates acquisition because it connects input, internal learner capacities, and output in productive ways. We need to distinguish between output as interaction with others and output as practice of forms and structures. L2 learners' implicit system develops as learners process the input they receive. Output promotes awareness and interaction with other learners but it does not play a direct role in the creation of the internal linguistic system. Conscious presentation and manipulation of forms through drills and output practice might help L2 learners to develop certain skills to use certain forms/structures correctly and accurately in controlled tasks but has very little impact on the development of the implicit system responsible for acquisition.

Is there an innate component in language acquisition?

For many linguists, language is a sophisticated system which develops unconsciously in the human mind. Language is therefore not considered as something relatively simple to learn via stimulus and reinforcement (behaviour), but as a very complex, mental and elaborate system which exists inside the mind. All humans possess innate knowledge of language universals and principles which regulate the acquisition of languages. These universal principles are modified and corrected in light of the input to which humans are exposed. We are not 'blank slates', but instead come to the learning of a language with a knowledge of language universals (innate knowledge) that guides our active processing of information to convert it into something useable at a given point in time. A number of claims have been made about this innate component of language and language acquisition. The first claim is that language learners somehow know how a linguistic feature works. They just know what is allowed and disallowed in a language. The second claim is that when learners are exposed to input, that input triggers a resetting mechanism which resets their parameters (if the first language of language learners is head-initial (position of verb) and they are learning another language that is head-final, input will trigger learners to re-set this parameter from head-initial to head-final).

How does the language system develop?

Language learners develop an internal language system. This system, as it develops, is neither the first language nor the second language, but something in-between that learners build from environmental data (input). Language development requires making connections between language forms and functions. The forms are morphological inflections and word order patterns. The functions are grammatical functions with specific semantic properties. A language system is slow to develop as learners' minds are constantly working on various aspects of language simultaneously. Only over time does the internal system build up and begin to resemble the second language. Language development is also stage-like and ordered-like. In the acquisition of structure there are stages that all learners go through regardless of their L1. There is no evidence that stages can be skipped or orders can be altered. Both stage-like and ordered second language development offer clear evidence that learners must possess internal mechanisms that process and organise language material over time in a systematic manner. Language learners create a language system in an organised way that seems little affected by external factors such as instruction and correction. The system is implicit and is principally guided by the learner's interaction with L2 input.

What is the role of instruction?

Instruction has a limited and constrained role in second language acquisition. However, it can be beneficial under certain conditions. Acquisition is an unconscious and implicit process, and learners acquire a second language through exposure to comprehensible and meaning-bearing input rather than learning grammar consciously through explicit grammatical rules. Language learners acquire grammatical features (e.g. morphemes) of a target language in a predictable order and this is regardless of their first language or the context in which they acquire them. Instruction is also constrained by developmental stages, as language learners follow a very rigid route in the acquisition of grammatical features. If instruction is targeted to grammatical features for which language learners are developmentally ready, then instruction can be beneficial in helping them to move faster along their natural route of development. Instruction might also have a facilitative role in helping learners to pay selective attention to form and form-meaning connections in the input. Learners make form-meaning connections from the input they receive as they connect particular meanings to particular forms (grammatical or lexical). Evidence in second language research shows that the route of acquisition cannot be altered. However, instruction might in certain conditions speed up the rate of acquisition. What are the conditions that might facilitate the speed in which languages are learned? A first condition is that language learners must be exposed to sufficient input. A second condition is that language learners must be developmentally ready for instruction to be effective. A third condition is that instruction must take into consideration how L2 learners process input.

Is there a role for individual difference?

The role of individual differences in second language acquisition has focused principally on constructs such as aptitude, working memory, and motivation. Language aptitude is related to the broader concept of human abilities covering a variety of cognitive-based learner differences. Working memory is an essential element in developing our ability to process linguistic data and it plays a central role in language processing (ability to process symbols, store capacity and integrate information) in both comprehension and the production of language. Motivation to acquire a second language includes three main elements: the effort undertaken by the individual to learn a language; the willingness to achieve a goal; the enjoyment in the task of learning a second language. These individual factors are certainly important constructs to measure learner's positive attitudes towards the learning of a language. However, they do not provide us with an understanding and explanations of the internal and universal processes and mechanisms involved in the acquisition of another language.

What do we know about SLA?

There are two competing accounts (domain-general and language-specific) in second language acquisition:

(a) Some scholars and researchers argue that language is like any other complex mental task such as reading, playing chess, and in general solving problems. Like any other complex mental phenomenon it is learned via the same domain-general mechanisms that enable us to learn how to program a computer or solve difficult puzzles.

(b) Other scholars and researchers instead, contend that language is special and it is not learned in the same way as other complex mental phenomena. Their claim is that humans are hardwired to learn language and have cognitive mechanisms specifically designed to deal with language. These are separate mechanisms from the domain-general one.

Theory and research in second language acquisition have emphasised the complexity of acquisition processes. How learners process language, how they intake it and the new language system develops, and how they access the information to communicate are key areas in this field of enquiry. Here is what we know about second language acquisition: (a) Language as mental representation is different from developing a language skill. Language is a complex, abstract and implicit system. (b) Second language acquisition is primarily a matter of developing implicit knowledge. (c) Input is the key ingredient in the process of acquisition. (d) L2 learners require extensive input exposure to build their internal language systems apart from some universal exceptions. (e) Input needs to be easily comprehended and message-oriented to be processed effectively by L2 learners. (f) L2 learners focus primarily on meaning when they process elements of the new language. Acquisition requires learners to make appropriate and efficient form–function connections (the relation between a particular form and its meaning/s). (g) Interaction with other speakers, negotiation of meaning and corrective feedback may facilitate acquisition. (h) L2 learners process linguistic features following a natural order and a specific sequence (i.e. they master different grammatical structures in a relatively fixed and universal order and they pass through a sequence of stages to master grammatical structure). (i) Instruction might have a facilitative role through input manipulation pedagogical interventions. The key principles of second language acquisition are:

- Second language acquisition involves the development of an implicit, abstract, and complex language system.
- The development of this system has the following characteristics: it is slow; it is order-like; it is stage-like; it consists of different processes; it is constrained by learner-internal mechanisms.
- Explicit knowledge does not turn into implicit knowledge. Skill acquisition is different from the creation of an implicit system. It is the implicit system that learners must tap into to create and produce language.
- The basic data for second language acquisition is comprehensible and meaningful input. Universal principles of language interact with input data.
- Instruction might have a facilitative role (the question is what type) on the rate of acquisition.

What is a principled and evidence-based approach to language teaching?

The existence of a variety of methods and approaches in language teaching does not mean that we should necessarily adopt one of them, or attempt to develop a new one which has characteristics derived from them. Instead, the overall suggestion made in this pocket guide is that we should consider a principled and evidence-based approach to language instruction. One that draws from theories and empirical research/evidence in second language acquisition and provides some effective options for instructors and instruction. Acquisition is input driven, stage and process-like, implicit, unconscious, and instruction has a limited and constrained role. A new approach to language instruction should address some of the main pedagogical questions raised by language instructors, and it should be guided and informed by theory and evidence. It is not what we think might work but what actually works based on evidence, and is effective in the language classroom, that we need to consider. If adopted, a principle- and evidence-based approach to language instruction will have the following characteristics:

- The language input provided in the classroom will be comprehensible and meaningful. L2 learners must be given the opportunity to interact and to be exposed to meaningful input.
- Grammar is not explained through rules or paradigms but is embedded in the input (manipulated input), and language learners should be engaged with grammar tasks moving from input to output practice. It is paramount to have a good understanding of the role and nature of language in order to approach the teaching of grammar.
- Vocabulary is practised taking into consideration the following: present new word repeatedly and frequently in the input; use meaning-bearing comprehensible input when processing new words; present words in an enhanced manner.
- Tasks become the main type of activities in the classroom and are based on a specific definition of communication. During language interactive tasks (e.g. information-exchange tasks, problem-solving tasks), learners have the opportunity to interpret input, interact with others, exchange information, negotiate meaning, and produce new language.
- Error correction is kept to a minimum. Teachers provide more exposure to correct input through recasts, and language learners are encouraged to self-repair.
- The role of the teachers is to set up language tasks and ensure that language learners have considerable exposure to language input and the opportunity to interpret, negotiate meaning and produce language for a specific purpose.
- Listening, Reading, Writing and Listening skills are better developed using a pre–while–post task approach.

Instructors must be encouraged to actively conduct their own investigations in the language classroom to test the effectiveness of all these pedagogical interventions. As we look at the future, language scientists need to continue to conduct research looking into how language is represented in the mind/brain, how it is comprehended and produced, and how universals and bilingualism affect the human mind/brain. The mission of researchers and practitioners is to change the idea and the myths that language is a list of rules, that a paradigm is the way language is represented in the mind/brain, that communication can be reduced to the Q/A paradigm, that explicitly teaching grammar and vocabulary is necessary or even beneficial, that practice makes perfect, that first-language transfer is the source of all learning problems, and that adults learn languages differently from children.

The way forward is to provide appropriate language teachers training for instructors, to change practices and policies as regard to language curriculum and language testing in schools and universities. Curriculum or language teaching materials must be genuinely informed by what we know about language and language acquisition. Language scientists have the responsibility to carry out appropriate and sound empirical research. Language scientists have started to investigate the brain signatures of second language acquisition by comparing different groups of learners undergoing different kinds of language instructions. They have been using machines and lab equipment (Eye-tracking, Self-paced tests, ERPs, and EEG systems) to test what happens to students' brains in real teaching/acquisition contexts. Very soon we will be in the position where we can predict whether acquisition of a second language is really taking place when using specific pedagogical interventions. We should continue to conduct neurolinguistics and psycholinguistic longitudinal and cross-sectional experiments in real language classes with real learners. Neuro/psycholinguistic-teaching research is the new quest for the 'Holy Grail'. We can now track the internalisation and development of language competence. This would widen the horizons of second language acquisition research to an extent that cannot be predicted now.

Read more about it

Benati, A. (2020) *Key Questions in Language Teaching*. Cambridge: Cambridge University Press.

Benati, A. (2014) Second language acquisition. In Fäcke, C. (ed.), *Language Acquisition* (179–97). New York: Mouton de Gruyter.

Chomsky, N. (1965) *Aspects of the Theory of Syntax*. Cambridge, MA: MIT Press.

Gass, S. and Selinker, L. (2008) *Second Language Acquisition: An Introductory Course*. New York: Routledge.

Hinkel, E. (2005) (ed.) *Handbook of Research in Second Language Teaching and Learning*. Mahwah, NJ: Lawrence Erlbaum Associates.

Keating, G. (2018) *Second Language Acquisition. The Basics*. New York: Routledge

Krashen, S.D. (1982) *Principles and Practice in Second Language Acquisition*. New York: Pergamon Press.

Larsen-Freeman, D. (2000) *Techniques and Principles in Language Teaching*. Oxford: Oxford University Press.

Long, M. (2007) *Problems in SLA*. Mahwah, NJ: Lawrence Erlbaum Associates.

Pienneman, M. and Kessler, J.-U. (2011) *Studying Processability Theory*. Amsterdam: John Benjamins.

VanPatten, B. (2010) Two faces of SLA: Mental representation and skill. *Journal of English Studies*, 10: 1–18.

VanPatten, B., Smith, M. and Benati, A. (2020) *Key Questions in Second Language Acquisition*: *An Introduction*. Cambridge: Cambridge University Press.

White, L. (2003) *Second Language Acquisition and Universal Grammar*. Cambridge: Cambridge University Press.

1 Age

Can we take a minute to think about this?

One of the key questions in second language acquisition research is: does age make a difference? A common belief is that children pick up another language faster than adults. If children are so special when it comes to learning another language, would it not be the case to assume that people should learn another language when they are still children? To make this assumption is to embrace the idea that humans go through a critical period for learning a language after which it is not possible to acquire another language. Critical period means that there is a limited time period for language acquisition. Is this true?

To answer this question, it is necessary to clarify what the nature and role of age in language acquisition actually is. Two questions have been raised in relation to the nature and role of age, and the second question is the consequence of the first one:

- If we believe that children engage with internal mechanisms which might not be available, does this mean that there is a 'cut off point' after which it is more difficult to learn another language?
- Would the existence of a critical period mean that adults cannot reach native-likeness?

The misleading view of the existence of a period after which humans find it more difficult to learn a language, or cannot learn a language, fails to account for the numerous L2 adult learners who appear to have achieved native-like proficiency. Adults achieving native-like proficiency is certainly a possibility.

What is the nature and role of age?

Is there a critical period for learning a language?

The concept of 'critical period' derives from first language acquisition research. The main concept of this hypothesis is that language can't be learned past a certain age. According to this view, if children are not exposed to sufficient linguistic input prior to a certain age (puberty), then language mechanisms responsible for learning is no longer available, and learning a language is not possible or is largely impaired. A common explanation for this view is the fact that language learners are not uniformly successful at learning in the way that first language learners are.

The concept of critical period finds support from research that suggests that children mainly rely on implicit processes to acquire languages, whereas post critical period learners rely on explicit processes. Because the linguistic mechanisms posited for children only work implicitly, then the conclusion is that post critical period second language learners are not engaging those mechanisms if they are learning explicitly. In other words, children and post critical period second language learners engage different learning mechanisms. Research around the role of a possible critical period affecting language acquisition has indicated three possible scenarios: (i) there is a critical period for learning a language; (ii) there is no critical period; (iii) there are various critical periods.

(i) Scholars supporting the view that there is a critical period in language learning largely base their view on the fact that second language (L2) learners are not uniformly successful at acquisition the way first language (L1) learners are. The main reason for this is that children rely largely on implicit processes for language development, whereas adult L2 learners rely on explicit processes. Because the linguistic mechanisms posited for children only work implicitly, then the conclusion is that post critical period adult learners are not engaging those mechanisms if they are learning explicitly. The so-called 'the younger = the better' hypothesis is supported by a number of studies comparing pre-puberty groups vs. post-puberty groups, has indicated that pre-puberty groups are better at learning than post-puberty groups.

(ii) Scholars supporting the view that there is no critical period in language learning offer evidence that non-natives can indeed obtain native-like ability (more later on this issue). They argue that adult L2 learners do have access to both universal grammar properties and the linguistic mechanisms guiding acquisition that are present in L1 acquisition. Research supporting this view has indicated that the loss of language ability is not linked to a particular period. A number of factors might be held responsible for a gradual decline of native-likeness. Putting this concept in another way, the earlier the age of acquisition, the more one is likely to be closer to native-likeness.

(iii) Some scholars have argued that a critical period view is not sustainable, and this position is held on the basis that language is componential in nature and it might be possible that some elements have critical periods and others not. In the case of universal grammar, it is possible that universal principles are still available to adult L2 learners but that new parameters are not. Once parameters are set when we learn our L1, certain values are lost and cannot be retrieved later. The conclusion is that there is no critical period for universals (principles inherent to all languages) but there is a critical period beyond which resetting parameters is impaired. It is difficult to support the view that a critical period truly exists as there is contradictory evidence investigating age as an indicator of successful language acquisition. Factors related to access to input and opportunities for interaction are important determining variables that might affect the rate and success of second language acquisition.

Learning a second language seems to be more difficult and less efficient than learning our first language during childhood. However, neurocognitive research, using event-related brain potentials, has demonstrated that adults normally display a similar real-time pattern of brain activation when processing a second language (natural or artificial) to native speakers when processing natural languages. Participants trained in the artificial languages, for example, showed two event-related brain potential components taken to reflect early automatic and late controlled syntactic processes, whereas untrained participants did not. This result challenges the common view that late L2 learners process language in a principally different way from native speakers. These findings demonstrate that a small system of grammatical rules can be syntactically instantiated by the adult speaker in a way that strongly resembles native-speaker sentence processing.

Can L2 adult learners reach native-likeness?

This is a question that has been researched extensively in second language research. The native language is considered to be the one humans acquire from birth. This is in contrast to languages acquired later. The term 'native-like' refers to whether or not L2 learners reach the same level of competence in an L2 such as the one they possess in their L1. As in the case of the critical period, there are different positions among scholars: (i) adult L2 learners cannot develop native-like L2 ability; (ii) adult L2 learners can develop native-like ability; (iii) adult L2 learners can develop native-like underlying competence in some if not all domains, but there may be problems in terms of the interface between underlying competence and production.

(i)   This position holds that L2 learners are unable to achieve native-like ability and the bulk of evidence comes from research on grammatical development as well as phonology (sound system and pronunciation). Typically, in this research, very advanced native-like L2 learners are compared with native speakers on a variety of grammatical features (e.g. tense, aspect, syntactic structure) using tests designed to tap the underlying competence of the participant. These are usually paper and pencil tests designed to get at intuitions about the language that native speakers typically possess, but more recent research has begun to examine processing and parsing (how learners create syntactic structure in real time while listening to or reading sentences). Research from this side of the question has shown, for example, that few if any native-like speakers demonstrate native-like underlying competence. Their scores on the tests of intuitions may yield scores that are significantly different from those of a group of native speakers. In terms of phonology, a number of studies suggest that non-natives cannot achieve native-like pronunciation. Second language adult learners 'can't' become native-like. Native-likeness decreases as the age of learning an L2 increases.

(ii) This position holds that L2 learners can become native-like. Research in support of this view has found that, in language tests, a significant number of non-natives were indistinguishable from natives.

(iii) Other research has suggested that learners can achieve native-likeness in some domains but not others, or that their underlying competence may be native-like but for some reason there is a disconnect between competence and performance.

Empirical research does yield clear evidence that non-natives can become native-like. At the same time, the research also suggests that most do not. Thus, native-likeness is possible but its probability is not high. The question is not whether learners can become native-like but why more do not. At the same time, we see something else emerging in the literature: that native-likeness is possible, but that it may be masked by matters unrelated to the focus of inquiry. Native-like mental representation is possible, but issues related to language production mask this. Although learning a second language as an adult is notoriously difficult, research has shown that adults can indeed attain native language-like brain processing and high proficiency levels.

What are the main points?

There might be some evidence to support the view that individuals before puberty tend to learn a language faster and more efficiently than other individuals who are in their post puberty period. However, there is also evidence that shows that there is no such a thing as a critical period. Children acquiring a second language engage in activities and behaviours conducive to acquisition. The answer might be that, in some cases, the mechanisms for language acquisition used by children might not work as well for adolescents and adults. However, it could also be true that there are certain environmental and social factors that have an effect on language acquisition.

Would time spent on the acquisition of a language be a major factor?

Would the type of exposure to the second language be a key factor?

Adults and adolescents might not have the same amount of time and type of exposure to language input as children learning a second language. As we explore some of the key terms and aspects of language acquisition and language teaching, the answer to these questions will become more explicit.

Meanwhile, the main points to keep in mind are:

- There might be a critical period for learning a language after which it is more complex to learn a second language. However, there is a view that only some elements of the language can be affected.
- There might be no such a thing as a critical period as we should consider certain environmental and social factors as responsible for a difference in learning experience between children, adolescents and adults.
- In examining the findings investigating the role of a critical period in language acquisition, we must conclude that conflicting results and other views have undermined the original claim that a critical period exists in second language acquisition. The critical period hypothesis fails to account for the numerous adult learners who appear to have achieved native-like proficiency.
- Adults achieving native-like proficiency is certainly a possibility.

What else can we read?

Birdsong, D. (1999) *Second Language Acquisition and the Critical Period Hypothesis*. Mahwah, NJ: Lawrence Erlbaum Associates.

Birdsong, D. (2005) Interpreting age effects in second language acquisition. In Kroll, J. and de Groot, A. M. B. (eds) *Handbook of Bilingualism: Psycholinguistic Approaches* (109–27). Oxford: Oxford University Press.

Muñoz, C. (2006) *Age and the Rate of Foreign Language Learning*. Clevedon: Multilingual Matters.

Singleton, D. (2007) The critical period hypothesis. Some problems. *Interlinguistica* 17: 48–56.

VanPatten, B. and Benati, A. (2015) *Key Terms in Second Language Acquisition*. London: Bloomsbury.

2   Communication

Can we take a minute to think about this?

Language instructors often discuss what communication is and how it can be implemented in the language classroom. However, the general understanding of the term communication is not always accurate or clear. A definition of the nature and role of communication in language acquisition and language teaching is of vital importance.

One of the main goals in language teaching is to ensure that L2 learners develop their communicative skills in the language they are studying. Language instructors concentrate most of their efforts in ensuring L2 learners speak in the classroom and interact with others. However, the lack of knowledge about what communication is and how it develops leads to the following misleading assumptions and practices:

- In most cases the common practice in language teaching is to facilitate the development of communicative skills based on the Question/Answer paradigm (Q/A), or open-ended questions type of activities.
- Most language textbooks contain activities that are so-called 'communicative'. For instance, L2 learners are asked to look at some pictures or a dialogue and then produce the target language following a specific pattern.
- Most language textbooks contain activities where language learners are asked to talk about a topic (e.g. describe a friend or a member of your family or talk about your weekend or your summer holiday, etc.). Work in pairs and describe what you did last summer and make sure you provide the following information:
  - Who you were with
  - Where you stayed
  - What you did
  - What you liked most.

The main purpose of these activities is language practice. The real purpose of activities like the ones described here is for L2 learners to practise a particular form (past tense in the case of the above example) and use specific and relevant vocabulary. The fact that L2 learners are working together and speaking does not mean they are communicating. In the case of role plays practice, for example, learners have to play a role. They are provided with role player cards containing concrete information and clear role descriptions so that they can play their roles with confidence following the instructions. Although role plays require L2 learners to express meaning, they fall short of being communicative. The meaning learners have been asked to express is not their own but of imaginary people in an imaginary setting. Very often, learners are playing an unreal role.

What is the nature and role of communication?

Communication cannot be equated with the Q/A paradigm, use of role plays or open-ended questions type of language practice. Communication instead can be defined as the expression, interpretation and negotiation of meaning for a specific purpose in a given context. It is crucial that we fully understand the nature and role of communication because we know that interaction promotes comprehension and comprehension promotes acquisition. Communicative tasks promote acquisition and provide a purpose for language use. A task can be used to achieve a specific lesson objective. Tasks (and not exercises or activities) should form the backbone of the curriculum. A definition and understanding of the nature of communication is also crucial for developing effective communicative skills.

Communication is the expression, interpretation, and negotiation of meaning for a specific purpose in a given context. Let's now examine the components of communication.

Expression and interpretation

Expression refers to any type of production during a communicative event. However, meaning can be expressed without the use of language (e.g. raising eyebrows, smiling, waving, eyes narrowing). In face-to-face interactions for example, people tend to use both oral and non-oral expression of meaning.

Communication is not one-sided, and there is always someone else expected to understand and interpret the message or the intent of the message we are trying to convey.

Negotiation of meaning

Negotiation of meaning shows up in a variety of ways:

> *Statement:* 'I'm sorry, but I don't understand'. 'Please, say it again'.
> *Comprehension check:* 'You know what I mean?'
> *Confirmation check:* 'Let me see if I got this right. You're saying that…'.
> *Gesture or look*: I spread my hands out with a look on my face that says 'Huh?'

All of above examples are ways in which interlocutors initiate meaning checks which can then lead to negotiation of meaning. Meaning refers to the information contained in the message we intend to convey. If someone says, for example, 'it's three o'clock', the literal meaning of the sentence is that is that it's three o'clock. However, meaning can also refer to someone's intent. Maybe the speaker who says 'It's three o'clock' is worried that someone else is taking too long to get ready as he/she might be unaware of the time.

Context and purpose

The construct of context refers to two principal aspects of communication: (i) the setting; (ii) the participants. Context is a powerful dimension of any communicative event as it constrains how people communicate. Being in a classroom, for example, is not the same thing as being at a dinner table at home with friends or family. Interacting with our doctor is not the same as interacting with our friends. The context always dictates the way we interact and communicate messages.

When we communicate we do so with a purpose. We don't use language or gestures or signs or anything else involved in communication without a specific reason. People generally use language for the following purposes:

- Psycho-social purpose: to establish and maintain personal relationships (e.g. saying 'hello', to invite someone out for dinner, to inquire about members of the family, etc.);
- Cognitive-informational purpose: to exchange information with someone and learn something new, to obtain information for a specific purpose.

In everyday life, these two major purposes of communication overlap and we often move back and forth between the two during an interaction. Communication between two or more people always has some purpose. People use language in order to accomplish something (e.g. getting directions from a passerby and going from A to B; discussing your birthday to organise a party, etc.). The question is: do language teachers engage L2 learners in communication in the language classroom? Considering the way very often languages are still taught, it would appear that L2 learners are not exposed to appropriate communicative activities where they are engaged in the interpretation, expression and negotiation of meaning. The activities in the language classroom are often constructed simply to practise language.

Does this type of practice look familiar to you? 'Interview your partner and find out what he or she did last night'.

The above activity is not communicative at all. If language instructors and L2 learners are not engaged in the expression and interpretation of meaning what they're doing is not communicative. In the above example, it seems that they are not communicating as they are simply going through the motions. One student says 'I studied', another one says 'I watched TV'. Neither of them is saying much and we're not even sure they're paying attention to each other. The main characteristics of this open-ended question exercise are:

- There is no focus on the interpretation and expression of meaning.
- The purpose is reduced to practise language.

The concept of communication is at the heart of language acquisition, and communicative language abilities develop as L2 learners engage in communication. Mechanical practice does little to foster language development and only fosters the development of what we call a learning-like behaviour. Real communication is about language use in context. L2 learners learn to communicate by practising communication and negotiate the language input as in the following interaction between a native speaker (NS) and non-native speaker (NSS):

NS: What did you do last weekend?
NNS: *Hum...?*
NS: Saturday, Sunday ... Did you enjoy?

Interaction can foster acquisition when a communication problem arises and L2 learners are engaged in resolving this problem through interaction and negotiation of meaning. Features of language are learned if they have been linked to real-world meaning. Communication is not simply a matter of question and answers but involves expression, interpretation and negotiation of meaning.

The communication act involves the expression, interpretation and negotiation of meaning in a context for a specific purpose. Interactive tasks might provide L2 learners with opportunities to interpret and express meaning. In addition, language tasks have an informational purpose.

Speaking is an interactive process of constructing meaning that involves producing, receiving and processing information. Speaking in another language is not only developing the ability to use grammar correctly and have access to vocabulary and pronounce words correctly (linguistic competence), but it is also the ability to understand when, why and in what ways to produce language (communicative competence).

Language learners must be engaged in communicative language tasks where they use language that is meaningful. All communicative tasks must ensure language learners develop their ability to share information, negotiate meaning and interact with others. Speaking tasks must be developed with the intention of promoting communication and communicative language use. A communication task is a classroom activity that has (a) an objective attainable only by interaction among participants; (b) a mechanism for structuring and sequencing interaction; and (c) a focus on meaning exchange.

A communication task is a learning endeavour that requires L2 learners to comprehend, negotiate, manipulate and produce the target language as they need to perform some set of work-plans. L2 learners must develop their ability to manage interaction as well as engage in the negotiation of meaning. The management of the interaction involves such things as when and how to take the floor, when to introduce a topic or change the subject, how to invite someone else to speak, how to keep a conversation going and so on. Negotiation of meaning refers to the skill of making sure the person you are speaking to has correctly understood you and that you have correctly understood them.

Assuming that our aim is to develop L2 learners' communicative skills, classroom interactive tasks that stimulate communication in the language classroom should be developed. The following points are what language instructors should first consider:

- Much of the time allocated to an oral task must be occupied by language learners' talk and not instructors' talk. Classroom discussion must not be dominated by a minority of talkative participants and all L2 learners must contribute evenly.
- L2 learners need to use an appropriate, comprehensible and accurate level of target language. An oral task requires some degree of real-time exposure.

How do we develop effective oral interactive tasks? A series of measures needs to be considered in order to achieve this:

- Language instructors should develop group oral communication tasks which increase L2 learners' talk time and at the same time lower the inhibitions of learners who are unwilling to speak in front of the full class. In group work, L2 learners perform a learning task through small-group interaction. One of the advantages of group interaction is that it can foster learner responsibility and independence, and it can contribute to effective and careful organisation/planning.
- Language instructors should base the oral communication task on easy and comprehensible language that will help L2 learners to produce target language with the minimum of hesitation.
- Language instructors should keep L2 learners speaking the target language and they should monitor the learners' use of the target language at all times during their tasks. L2 learners should be allowed to initiate communication, and speaking tasks should involve negotiation for meaning. Positive corrective feedback on learners' performance should be carefully provided.

- Language instructors should choose an interesting and familiar topic which enables L2 learners to use and tap into their ideas from their own experience and knowledge.
- Language instructors should provide clear instruction to accomplish the communication task. In group or pair-work everyone in the group contributes to the discussion. A chairperson to each group is appointed to regulate participation. The role of the teacher is as 'a resource person' and 'architect' as she/he structures the task but is not responsible for its final accomplishment. L2 learners must take initiative and responsibility to complete the task. Language learners need to take the initiative and make decisions in order to communicate successfully.
- Language instructors should create a classroom environment where students have real-life authentic communication, and meaningful tasks that promote speaking skills. This can occur when students collaborate in groups to achieve a goal or to complete a task. L2 learners must be given a task where they need something to talk about and someone to talk to.
- Language instructors should develop a communication task that is essentially goal-oriented and that requires the group or pair to achieve an objective that is usually expressed by an observable result, such as brief notes or lists, a rearrangement of jumbled items, a drawing, a spoken summary.

In developing interactive communicative tasks, language instructors should adopt the following guidelines:

- Identify a desired information outcome
- Identify information sources
- Create and sequence concrete tasks for learners to complete
- Build in linguistic support.

Interactive communicative tasks should substitute traditional oral practice where L2 learners are asked to talk about a specific topic 'How do you spend your free time and over the weekend?' In the so-called open ended questions exercise, L2 learners have very little to talk about and few opportunities to interact.

Identify a desired information outcome

This is the first guideline to consider in developing an effective interactive communicative tasks. The main informational goal of the task needs to be determined. In other words, language instructors need to establish what specific questions L2 learners will be able to answer at the end of the task.

Identify information sources

Information that L2 learners need to exchange generates from two main sources: from themselves (e.g. their views, their opinions, etc.); and from outside sources (e.g. texts, programs. etc.).

Create and sequence concrete tasks for learners to complete

Once goals are established, the interactive communicative task is made of different steps/stages. Steps/stages are set so that L2 learners can meet the main goals of the task.

Build in linguistic support

L2 learners need to be provided with the appropriate linguistic support to complete the task. The question language instructors need to ask is: Do they have the sufficient vocabulary to complete the various steps of the task?

What are the main points?

- Communication cannot be equated with questions and answers (Q/A) practice.
- Communication can be defined as the expression, interpretation, and negotiation of meaning in a given context for a specific purpose.
- Interaction fosters acquisition when a communication problem arises and L2 learners are engaged in resolving it through interaction and negotiation of meaning.
- Tasks promote acquisition and provide a purpose for language use. A communicative interactive task is a learning endeavour that requires L2 learners to comprehend, negotiate, manipulate and produce the target language as they need to perform some set of work plans.

- Interactive tasks are a good example of communication tasks and should be a substitute for traditional oral practice.

What else can we read?

Benati, A. (2020) *Key Questions in Language Teaching*. Cambridge: Cambridge University Press.

Lee, J. (2000) *Tasks and Communicating in Language Classrooms*. New York: McGraw-Hill.

Lee, J. and VanPatten, B. (2003) *Making Communicative Language Teaching Happen*. New York: McGraw-Hill.

Long, M. (2015) *Second Language Acquisition and Task-based Language Teaching*. Malden, MA: Wiley-Blackwell.

Savignon, S (2005) *Communicative Competence. Theory and Classroom Practice*. New York: McGraw-Hill.

VanPatten, B. (2003) *From Input to Output*. NJ: McGraw-Hill.

3   Corrective Feedback

Can we take a minute to think about this?

Corrective feedback refers to the response that L2 learners receive regarding the errors they might make in language production. Do we need to correct errors? Is it true that failing to correct an error would have negative effects on language development? There is a belief that correcting errors immediately as they occur has a positive impact on language learning. This concept stems from the behaviourist's view that L2 learners might develop bad habits which must be immediately corrected.

Correcting errors is characterised by an overt and clear indication of the existence of an error and the provision of the target-like reformulation and can take two forms: explicit correction; and metalinguistic feedback. (i) In explicit correction, language teachers provide both positive and negative evidence by clearly saying that what L2 learners have produced is erroneous. (ii) In metalinguistic feedback the focus of conversation with L2 learners is diverted towards rules or features of the target language. Metalinguistic feedback is divided into three subcategories: metalinguistic comments, metalinguistic information and metalinguistic questions. The least informative one is metalinguistic comments which only indicate the occurrences of an error. Metalinguistic information not only indicates the occurrences or location of the error but also offers some metalanguage that alludes to the nature of the error. Metalinguistic questions point to the nature of the error but attempt to elicit the information from the learner. Metalinguistic feedback provides the non-native speaker (NNS) with a metalinguistic cue in the input and/or metalinguistic feedback about the correctness of an utterance.

NNS: I watch a good film at the weekend.
NS: You need to use the verb in the past tense (metalinguistic cue).
NNS: I watch a good film at the weekend.
NS: Watched is the past tense (metalinguistic feedback and correction).

One misleading belief of instructors is that L2 learners come to a second language with bad habits in the L1 which need to be corrected. Therefore, if errors occur, instructors should correct them immediately. What emerges from research is that any form of explicit correction of errors *has no long-term effect*. Empirical research on error correction in the form of overt correction does not have a measurable impact in second language acquisition. It might cause some temporary effects and reinforce our conscious knowledge about the target language, however *it does not* affect our internal implicit language system. The lack of knowledge about what theory and research is telling us about the nature and role of error correction leads to misleading claims and misunderstanding:

- In most cases the common error correction practice in language teaching includes explicit error correction by consciously drawing learner's attention to the error and teaching L2 learners how 'to say it right'. However, research on corrective feedback and language development has demonstrated that this type of error correction is not really effective in the long run. L2 learners learn language mainly through exposure to meaningful and comprehensible input. Error correction might put learners on the defensive, as they try to avoid making mistakes.
- Explicit error correction might have a temporary effect on L2 learners' performance in terms of monitoring more what they are saying. However, this kind of explicit corrective feedback practice does not have any effect on their internal implicit language system and/or does not cause any lasting changes in speech production.

It is therefore necessary to clarify whether there are more effective forms of implicit and indirect error correction. Indirect error correction might be useful where it is provided as part of a communicative interaction. Feedback might be provided not by correcting the error *per se* but by focusing on the information that L2 learners are trying to convey. Can we provide effective corrective feedback as part of a communicative interchange between a language learner and a native speaker?

What is the nature and role of corrective feedback?

Interactional corrective feedback refers to feedback that learners receive on their erroneous or inappropriate utterances during [conversational] interaction. The example below is a typical corrective feedback exchange.

1 Instructor: What did you do on the weekend?
2 Learner: We went at the cinema (trigger).
3 Instructor: Oh, you went to the cinema (feedback).
4 Learner: Yes, went to the cinema (uptake).

Corrective feedback (indirect and implicit) is in antithesis to direct and explicit error correction and should be considered a facilitative tool in language learning and teaching. It refers to utterances from a language instructor (NS = native speaker) or a non-native speaker (NNS) which indicates that the learner's output is not correct. In the case of a breakdown in communication between interlocutors, corrective feedback in natural conversations might be useful. This feedback is usually provided though different conversational interventions and negotiation strategies (e.g. clarification requests, confirmation checks, recast) which take place during an interaction.

In providing corrective feedback, language instructors and L2 learners should consider the following questions: (i) do we need to correct language errors? If the answer is yes, (ii) what is the best way to correct errors?

Do we need to correct language errors?

Overall, research on direct and explicit error correction has demonstrated that it is not effective as it does not (i) have an impact on L2 learners' implicit system, and (ii) it does not increase their ability to correctly string together language elements in a sentence. However, the question is not whether or not we should correct errors, but how we should do it.

Interactional input refers to input received during interaction where there is some kind of communicative exchange/classroom interaction involving the learner and at least one other person. Through these interactions, L2 learners have the advantage of being able to negotiate meaning and make some conversational adjustments when necessary if there is a breakdown in communication. How L2 learners are led to notice things can happen in several ways.

Input modifications happen when the other speaker adjusts his or her speech due to perceived difficulties in learner comprehension. Learners can then receive some corrective feedback. The other speaker indicates in some way that the learner has produced something non-native-like. A typical interactional feedback exchange might be as follows:

NS: Where did you go last summer?
NNS: I was in vacation.
NS: Oh, where did you go on vacation?
NNS: I was on vacation in Italy.

L2 learners sometimes request clarifications or repetitions if they do not understand the message of the language input they are exposed to. In an attempt to facilitate comprehension, one person can request the other to modify his/her utterances. Various kinds of interactional feedback have been used for modifying interaction. The most common are:

*Clarification reques*ts can be defined as expressions used to clarify learners' utterances (e.g. What did you say?);
Confirmation checks are used by learners and teachers when it is not clear what has been said (e.g. Did I understand correctly?);
Comprehension checks are used when one speaker is not convinced that the other speaker has understood what has been said (e.g. Do you know what I mean?);
Recast is the reformulation of a speaker's erroneous utterance.

Although the use of the application of corrective feedback is useful to negotiate meaning and expose learners to positive evidence in the input, it has a limited effect on second language acquisition. From an interaction perspective, corrective feedback can be beneficial as it provides indirect information about the grammaticality of the utterances as well as additional positive evidence which may otherwise be absent from the input. From a second language acquisition perspective, corrective feedback might not affect the development of L2 learners' internal and implicit language system.

How should we correct errors?

A number of corrective feedback types have been researched and proposed to suggest how errors should be corrected: recast; elicitation; clarification requests; and non-verbal feedback. These types of interactional feedback have some facilitative effects in generating student self-repairs and self-correction.

Corrective feedback can occur in two different ways: (i) reformulations; and (ii) elicitation.

Reformulations are those corrective feedback pedagogical interventions such as recast when L2 learners are provided with the correct form.

Elicitations refer to others corrective feedback pedagogical interventions which do not provide L2 learners with the correct form. For example, corrective feedback such as clarification requests do not provide L2 learners with target like forms. Learners are encouraged to repair their own errors by providing them with prompts and by giving them a chance to reformulate their utterance.

There are also two main types of learners' uptake (learners' reaction following language teachers' feedback): (i) uptake that produces a new sentence still needing repair; and (ii) uptake that produces a repair of the error on which the language instructor's feedback is focused.

Recast

In second language acquisition 'recast' can be defined as a teacher's reformulation of all or part of a learner's utterance, minus the error. Two main classification of recast have been proposed: (a) simple recast deals with minimal changes to the language learner's utterance; (b) complex recast is concerned with providing the language learner with substantial additions. Recast is used by language instructors to make sure that the learner becomes aware that something is wrong in their speech production. Below is one example of how recast can be used:

NNS: It bugs me when a bee sting me.
NS: Oh, when a bee stings me.
NNS: Stings me.
NS: Do you get stung often?

In the above example, the non-native speaker produces a sentence which contains an error. The native speaker (e.g. language instructor) provides recast by reformulating learner's incorrect form into a correct form. The successful correction made by the non-native speakers is called uptake. The native speaker continues the interaction in the attempt not to break the flow of communication. The degree of explicitness in using this type of corrective feedback would also vary depending on the use of intonational signals. In the example below the added stress makes the recast more explicit:

> NNS: It bugs me when a bee sting me.
> NS: Oh, when a bee STINGS me.
> NNS: Stings me.
> NS: Do you get stung often?

Recast is an interactional and implicit corrective feedback pedagogical intervention which can be implemented in different ways. The native speaker reformulates the non-native speaker utterance with the intention of correcting one or multiple errors. There is no general agreement among language researchers and practitioners regarding the effectiveness of recast.

Elicitation

Elicitation is a corrective feedback pedagogical intervention that prompts the L2 learner to self-correct and may be accomplished in one of three following ways during face-to-face interaction: (i) reformulations of an ill-formed utterance; (ii) use of open questions; (iii) use of strategic pauses to allow a learner to complete an utterance. Each of these vary in their degree of implicitness or explicitness. With the direct elicitation, the native speaker attempts to elicit relevant information from the non-native speaker. There is no correction but an opportunity for self-repair (see example below).

> NNS: And when the young girl arrive, ah, beside the old woman.
> NS: When the young girl …?

Clarification Request

Corrective feedback that carries questions indicating that the utterance has been ill-formed or misunderstood and that a reformulation or a repetition is required is called clarification request. Clarification requests, unlike explicit error correction and recast, can be more consistently relied upon to generate modified output from L2 learners. Clarification requests do not supply L2 learners with any information concerning the type or location of the error but offer the opportunity for self-repair. Clarification requests occur when there is a breakdown of communication between two speakers and one speaker asks the other speaker to clarify his/her utterance. Phrases such as 'sorry?' or 'what did you say? or 'say it again, please', provide the learner with an opportunity to clarify and/or make his utterance more accurate. Below is an example of a clarification request.

NNS: I can find no [ruddish].
NS: I'm sorry. You couldn't find what?

Nonverbal feedback

Nonverbal feedback is also another form of corrective feedback. Body movements and signals such as gestures, facial expressions, rolling your eyes, crossing your arms, head, hand, and finger movements are all different forms of feedback. Nonverbal feedback is feedback that the teacher provides to students with their actions (e.g. smiling, patting a student's shoulder, etc.).

Although there are no answers yet from individual studies about which type of feedback is more effective, important insights can be drawn from current research:

- Feedback might be more effective by using additional intonational prompts.
- Feedback is more effective when targeting a single linguistic feature at a time.
- The effects of feedback may not be immediate but gradual.
- Correct the same error on different occasions so that the learner can have enough exposure to the correct form.
- Not all grammar forms and structures respond equally to instruction and corrective feedback.
- Learners may notice lexical errors more effectively than morphosyntactic errors.
- The acquisition of some grammatical structures may follow developmental sequences. Learners learn when they are developmentally ready.

Therefore, for corrective feedback to be effective, teachers should match the feedback with learners' developmental stages. However, there is not yet adequate information about developmental sequences to guide teachers' decisions.

What are the main points?

The main question is not whether language instructors should correct errors, but how corrective feedback should be provided. Corrective feedback might play a facilitative role in language learning if a learner's attention can be drawn to the properties of the language through exposure to input. A key objective in corrective feedback is that it should generate the possibility for L2 learners to self-repair alongside some form of uptake.

- Two key questions addressed: should we correct errors? How should we correct errors?
- Corrective feedback might play a facilitative role in enabling self-repair and uptake.
- Corrective feedback pedagogical interventions (although one size does not fit all) should elicit student-generated repairs.
- There are two main types of corrective feedback available to language instructors: (i) reformulations; and (ii) elicitations.
- Research findings on the role of corrective feedback have indicated the following:
    - Corrective feedback should be used to elicit student-generated repairs.
    - Single linguistic features (one at a time) should be targeted.
    - One size does not fit all.
    - Self-correction should be encouraged.
    - Corrective feedback should generate some form of uptake.

What else can we read?

Doughty, C. and Williams, J. (1998) *Focus on Form in Classroom Second Language Acquisition.* New York: Cambridge University Press.

Lyster, R. and Ranta, L. (1997) Corrective feedback and learner uptake: Negotiation of form in communicative classrooms. *Studies in Second Language Acquisition*, 19: 37–66. https://doi.org/10.1017/s0272263197001034

Long, M. (2007) *Problems in SLA*. New York: Lawrence Erlbaum Associates.

Nassaji, H. (2015) *The Interactional Feedback Dimension in Instructed Second Language Learning*. London: Bloomsbury.

Sheen, Y. (2011) *Corrective Feedback, Individual Differences and Second Language Learning*. New York: Springer.

4 Explicit and Implicit

Can we take a minute to think about this?

One of the clear misunderstandings in second language acquisition and language teaching is the role and nature of explicit and implicit knowledge/learning. The lack of understanding about these key constructs leads to a number of misleading claims:

- Explicit knowledge turns into implicit knowledge.
- Explicit knowledge about formal properties of language affects acquisition.

Explicit knowledge of language is defined as conscious knowledge. It is often verbalisable knowledge about language such as to talk about something in the past, you add *-ed* to the stem at the end of the verb. Implicit knowledge is defined as unconscious knowledge and it is not verbalisable. It can be described as the ability to understand or supply *played* and not *play* in contexts that require the use of past tense in English, and to do so without a conscious effort to retrieve the form.

Explicit knowledge does not turn into implicit knowledge. However, the misleading view that it does has some consequences. In traditional grammar instruction, for instance: (i) language teachers instruct L2 learners about some specific grammatical forms (explicit information often using paradigms); (ii) L2 learners practise the target forms through mechanical practice; and (iii) at the end, language teachers assess them using paper-pencil tests. There are *two problems* with this type instruction aimed at developing explicit knowledge: (1) it does not correspond to the way language develops in our mind/brain; (2) it does not correspond to the way L2 learners process information.

What is the nature and role of implicit and explicit knowledge?

Developing explicit knowledge is the ability to consciously process language with the intention of finding out whether the language contains regularities and, if so, to work out the concepts and rules with which these regularities can be captured. Developing implicit knowledge is the unconscious input processing of language.

There are two positions on the role of implicit and explicit knowledge in second language acquisition. The first view (i) is that second language acquisition is exclusively implicit. The second view (ii) is that second language acquisition consists of both implicit and explicit learning.

The first position (i) argues that second language acquisition is implicit. A clear distinction is made between acquisition and learning. Acquisition involves implicit learning and results in the development of underlying competence, while learning involves explicit learning and results in a learned system, available for monitoring. We refer here to a Chomskyan definition of competence, which is the implicit and abstract knowledge of language, an interaction of abstract principles and processes of language that make sentences look the way they look to us.

Scholars from a universal grammar perspective are in support of the first position (i), and would also argue that the development of underlying competence is the result of the interaction of processed input data with universal and innate principles and parameters which we all possess. This interaction happens outside of learner awareness. One of the key claims of this theoretical perspective is that languages is a complex and abstract system which develops in the human mind. All humans possess innate knowledge of language universals and principles which regulate the acquisition of languages. These universals and principles are modified and corrected in the light of the input to which humans are exposed. Researchers within this theoretical framework have been concerned with how languages are represented in the mind (mental representation of language) and how learners come to know more about a language than that which they have been exposed to (poverty of the stimulus). In other words, they sometime know how a linguistic feature works, what is grammatical or ungrammatical, without having been exposed to that particular feature. When learners are exposed to input, that input resets their internal abstract principles. For example, L1 English learners would need to modify the principle that language is 'head initial' (*Alessandro speaks Japanese*) to the principle of 'head final' when learning Japanese (*Alessandro Japanese speaks* or *Japanese Alessandro speaks*). All humans have universal features of language which constrain the acquisition of grammar.

From a psychological perspective scholars would also argue that acquisition is largely implicit and it is the result of unconscious processing of linguistic data in the input. Acquisition is a dynamic process in which a number of elements (e.g. regularities, frequencies, associations, L1, interactions, brain, society and cultures) operate and are responsible for the emergence of and development of the second language. According to this theoretical perspective, explicit processes do not result in the developing of an implicit linguistic system. Frequency and regularity are key factors and language and its properties emerge as the result of simple cognitive learning mechanisms interacting with data from the environment. L2 learners are actively and consciously involved in trying to learn things such as verb endings, nominal inflections, and rules.

The second position (ii) suggests that second language acquisition involves both implicit and explicit learning. From a skill-theory perspective humans develop explicit knowledge about the language first and, subsequently, through adequate practice and exposure move into implicit knowledge. Second language acquisition entails going from controlled mode of operation (declarative knowledge) to automatic mode (procedural knowledge) through repeated practice. Learning begins with declarative knowledge (information is gathered and stored), and slowly becomes procedural (people move towards the ability to perform with that knowledge). Declarative knowledge involves acquisition of isolated facts and rules (*e.g. knowing that a car can be driven*). Procedural knowledge requires practice and involves processing of longer units and increasing automatisation (*e.g. knowing how to drive a car*). This position addresses issues related to the way people develop fluency and accuracy. Learners need to be taught explicitly and need to practise the various grammatical features and skills (develop accuracy) until they are well established (fluency). According to this view, both explicit and implicit processes are at work in second language acquisition. The view is that L2 learners may notice linguistic features in the input and need some kind of conscious awareness for them to acquire the linguistic features of the target language.

What are the main points?

- Second language acquisition is largely implicit in nature as it involves implicit learning. However, this does not mean that L2 learners, especially adults, do not attempt to engage explicit learning in some way.
- Language competence is different from language performance. Competence is the implicit and abstract knowledge of a language possessed by native speakers. It is implicit because we are unaware of this knowledge and are unable to articulate its contents. It is abstract because it does not consist of rules such as 'verbs must agree with their subjects', but of other syntactic operations that yield sentences that can be described as having verbs that agree with their subjects. Performance, instead, refers to how people use language in concrete situations.
- L2 learners come to know much more than what they have been taught, have practised, or even been exposed to. The conclusion of many scholars is that this knowledge is the result of the interaction of universal principles with data from the environment; that is, input. Because internal mechanisms operate outside of awareness, only implicit learning can be involved.
- Any aspects of language that are the result of the interaction of innate and universal principles that govern language with the input data are acquired via implicit learning.

What else can we read?

DeKeyser, R.M. (2007) *Practice in a Second Language. Perspectives from Applied Linguistics and Cognitive Psychology*. Cambridge: Cambridge University Press.

Gass, S.M., Behney, J. and Plonsky, L. (2013) *Second Language Acquisition: An Introductory Course*. New York: Routledge.

VanPatten, B. (2016) Why explicit knowledge cannot turn into implicit knowledge. *Foreign Language Annals*, 49: 650–57. https://doi.org/10.1111/flan.12226

VanPatten, B. and Benati, A. (2015) *Key Terms in Second Language Acquisition*. London: Bloomsbury.

5   Focus on Form

Can we take a minute to think about this?

The current lack of knowledge and misinterpretations about how we learn a grammatical system of a language, and how we should teach grammar, has led to confusion and a number of misleading claims:

- Grammar is often presented through long and elaborated explanations (paradigms) of the grammatical rules of the target language.
- Paradigms are provided (lists and tables containing rules) and followed by mechanical output practice (written and oral exercises/drills) where the main focus is to practise the grammatical rules to develop accuracy.
- Grammar instruction is usually provided following a particular sequence which goes from mechanical to communicative drills practice.

Most language textbooks provide activities and exercises following a traditional approach when it comes to the teaching of grammar. The grammar section of these books is generally characterised by paradigmatic explanations. The paradigmatic explanation is followed by mechanical and drill practice. In this type of mechanical practice, real life situations are completely ignored and practice is implemented in a completely decontextualised way.

'Today we are going to learn about past tense forms. Does anyone know what the past tense is, how it is formed and how we use it? (silence from the class) Well, the past tense in Italian is formed by … (present the class with a paradigm of past tense). For example in this sentence we add/change … (quizzical look from students)…What is the past tense of the verb "to go"? If I need to say "Yesterday I went to the cinema with a friend" how do you say this in Italian? (one student ventures an answer) …'

Drills are problematic for two main reasons:

(a) They force L2 learners to produce grammatical forms before they are capable of comprehending the forms, which leads to incorrect generalisations and overuse of the form when not necessary. Learners need the opportunity to comprehend language before being able to use it accurately.

(b) They don't allow learners to make form-meaning connections in comprehension and production. The idea that acquiring grammar can be simply achieved by learning about the grammatical rules of a target language and by practising those rules through production tasks (very often mechanical and traditional) has been challenged by many scholars in the field of second language acquisition and language teaching. The use of explicit information and drill practice does not foster the acquisition of another language and plays a very small role. The question to address is: what should we do then?

Firstly, we must familiarise ourselves with current research and theory on the role of grammar instruction in second language acquisition. There is enough evidence to suggest that, on one hand, instruction has a limited role and, on the other hand, that a focus on grammar might have a facilitative role if we devise grammar tasks that enhance the grammatical features in the input first before we move to output practice.

Secondly, we need to acknowledge that despite what L2 learners bring to the task of acquisition, a variety of internal mechanisms and traits which effectively override most instructional efforts, the more researchers learn about what L2 learners do with input and how they do it, the closer they come to understanding the possibilities of instructional effects. Beneficial effects have been found on particular kinds of instructional interventions (focus on form); those that were both input oriented and meaning-based. These pedagogical interventions aim to manipulate the input L2 learners receive, and include instructional treatments such as text enhancement, structured input, and input flood.

What is the nature and role of focus on form?

Focus on form is a term which has been sometimes used to express different meanings. A clear distinction between 'focus on form' and 'focus on forms' should be made. Focus on forms is a term used to describe a type of pedagogical intervention that focuses on the explicit teaching of specific linguistic forms (one at the time) in a target language (e.g. discrete-point grammar presentation and practice). Focus on form can be described as involving a focus on meaning and a focus on form. During focus on form, L2 learners' attention is being focused on specific linguistic properties of the target language in the course of a communicative activity. More broadly 'focus on form' can be described as any pedagogical intervention aimed at drawing L2 learners' attention to the linguistic properties of a language through exposure to meaningful input.

Language is something internal, not external to the L2 learners. Each and every one of us creates a mental representation we call language. We create an abstract and complex system even though we don't know this. This is also why it is implicit. We know we have language in our heads, but we don't really know what the contents are. Language as mental representation is therefore too abstract and complex to teach and learn explicitly. Explicit rules and paradigms cannot be equated to this abstract and complex system because the two things are completely different. This implication stems from the fact that there is no internal mechanism that can convert explicit textbook rules into implicit mental representation of language. What winds up in the human mind has no resemblance to anything on textbook pages, or traditional grammar rules. The question is: can focus on form facilitate language development? Empirical evidence on the role of instruction in second language acquisition has led us to three basic facts:

- Instruction does not affect the stage-like or the ordered nature of acquisition. That is, instruction does not allow learners to skip stages or alter ordered acquisition. Learners seems to follow a particular order in the acquisition of language morphemes (e.g. English verbal inflections are acquired following this order: progressive *-ing* – regular tense *-ed* – third person singular *-s*. There are also certain stages (see table below) L2 learners follow in acquiring syntactic structures (e.g. negation, question formation).

Stages of acquisition: English negation

Stage	Description	Example
1	'No' is in front of (not attached to) verbs or nouns, sentence initial	*No eat that*
2	'No' moves after the subject of the sentence, and in front of (not attached) to verbs or nouns; 'don't' appears as an alternative to 'no'	*I no eat that*
3	Negation is attached to verbs, modals negated	*I can't eat that*
4	'Do' with attached negation	*I don't eat that*
		She didn't eat that

- There are internal constraints on acquisition. Something inside the learner's mind/brain processes and organises language in ways that can't be manipulated by outside forces such as instruction and practice.
- Input provides the data for acquisition. Instruction as input manipulation can facilitate language processing. Input manipulation refers to how language can be restructured so that L2 learners can be exposed to grammatical properties of a target language.

Overall, research investigating the role of focus on form in second language acquisition has indicated the need for a grammar component in second language instruction. The question is how this component should be provided. Focus on form involves reactive use of a wide variety of pedagogic procedures to draw learners' attention to linguistic problems in context, as they arise during communication. Focus on form has become a set of pedagogical interventions designed to draw L2 learners' attention to a linguistic form in a communicative context. The focus on form can be either pre-planned focusing on a particular form or it can be incidental as L2 learners engage in meaning-based activities. During a focus on form intervention the linguistic elements are dealt with either intensively (systematically) or extensively (incidentally), but the primary focus always lies on communication.

What are the main types of focus on form?

Input enhancement is a pedagogical intervention that aims at helping L2 learners to notice specific forms in the input. Enhanced input is input that has been altered typologically to enhance the saliency of target forms. Input enhancement is an input-based focus on form type of instruction that exposes L2 learners to comprehensible input and, at the same time, draws their attention to a specific linguistic property of the target language. Input enhancement varies in terms of explicitness and elaboration. One type of input enhancement focus on form type consists of modifying a text so that a particular target item would appear over and over again. In this way, the text will contain many exemplars of the same feature (input flood). A different type would consist of underlying, bolding or capitalising a specific grammatical item (providing typographical cues) in a text (textual enhancement). Textual enhancement is specifically used to make particular features of written input more salient with the scope to help learners notice these forms and eventually make appropriate form-meaning connections. The main characteristic of textual enhancement is to highlight the form in the text (e.g. bolding, underlying) while keeping learner's attention on meaning. No metalinguistic explanation is provided during input enhancement. A review of the main empirical evidence measuring the relative effects of textual enhancement provides the following insights. (i) Overall the effects of textual enhancement are positive in terms of increasing L2 learners' level of attention to a form. The majority of empirical evidence confirms that typographical enhancement increases the amount of attention paid to the target items. (ii) A number of factors might constrain the effects of input enhancement on the acquisition of grammar: proficiency level, the developmental stage and the degree of readiness of the learner; the type of linguistic feature chosen; and the intensity of the treatment.

Input flood is a type of input enhancement where the input L2 learners receive is saturated with the form that L2 learners should notice. The main characteristic of input flood is that the input L2 learners receive must be modified so that it contains many instances of the same form. The main purpose of this type of focus on form is to help L2 learners to notice the form embedded in the input. Another type of input enhancement is aural enhancement. This implicit type of focus on form involves the manipulation of listening materials with the aim of making specific linguistic forms more salient in the input. It can include increased volume, slower pace, or short pauses added before and/or after the target items. A review of the main empirical evidence measuring the relative effects of input flood provides the following insights: (i) input flood is an effective pedagogical intervention at developing L2 learners' implicit knowledge; (ii) input flood effectiveness is affected by factors such as the length of the treatment and the nature/complexity of the linguistic feature; (iii) input flood might increase the chances that L2 learners initially notice a specific target form in the input language they are exposed to.

Structured input is a type of focus on form used primarily to facilitate, at input-level, the connection of a linguistic feature to its meaning. Form-meaning connections are the relationship learners make between referential meaning and the way it is encoded linguistically. For example, when learners hear the sentence, *I played tennis in the park*, and understand that *played* means the action is in the past, a form-meaning connection is made. In structured input, L2 learners are required to simultaneously focus on form to get meaning so that they improve their ability to process the right information and make the right form-meaning connections during comprehension. This is a different function from simply noticing a form in the input, as noticing simply means to be consciously aware that the form is there. For example, L2 learners might hear the word *played* and notice that it is different from either *plays* or *playing*. However, they might not immediately connect the ending (e.g. verbal inflection *-ed*) with the concept that the action has already taken place (past event). Enhancing a feature in the input might help L2 learners to notice that feature, but it does not necessarily mean that L2 learners make appropriate form-meaning connections. Structured input practice pushes learners away from non-optimal processing strategies so that they are more likely to make correct form-meaning connections or parse sentences (compute basic structure in real time) appropriately during comprehension. Overall, the main findings from research measuring the effects of structured input on the interpretation and the processing of a specific target form or structure has revealed the following: (i) structured input is an effective type of focus on form; (ii) learners with different first languages (L1s) and backgrounds make consistent gains in interpretation and production tests at sentence and discourse-level; (iii) the effects of structured input are consistent, durative, and measurable for different languages and processing problems; (iv) L2 learners who receive training in one type of processing strategy for one specific form transfer the use of that strategy to other forms without further focus on form.

One issue to consider is whether specific forms of structures benefit with a particular type of focus on form. The answer is that we should look at the specific characteristic of a particular form/or structure. The subjunctive, for example, is not a frequent feature in the input. In addition, it is made redundant by the meaning indicated in the main clause (e.g. doubt). It is therefore a form with low communicative value. Because of this, structured input practice might be the most appropriate type of focus on form to use. Multiple factors might explain the particular difficulties in acquiring a structure and therefore the most appropriate pedagogical intervention can be chosen.

What about vocabulary?

In traditional instruction vocabulary is often learnt by heart, and there is time assigned for learning specific words by memorising and mechanically learning words. In a more acquisition-driven approach to language instruction, all words and lexical items would need to be embedded in the input in a frequent and repeated manner. Based on empirical research in second language acquisition, the following principles would promote effective vocabulary acquisition.

(a) The first principle is to develop a vocabulary acquisition task to target what vocabulary learners are going to be exposed to.

(b) The second principle is to present new words frequently and repeatedly in the input. There's a lot of research suggesting that frequency and repetition is really useful.

(c) The third principle is to promote incidental vocabulary learning. Incidental vocabulary learning is when L2 learners pick up new words when they are still exposed to them in the input and, again, preferably multiple times, frequently and repeatedly.

(d) The fourth principle is to use meaning-bearing comprehensible input when presenting new words.

(e) The final principle is to present new words in an enhanced manner. Most research on input enhancement has – to date at least – focused on enhancement for the acquisition of grammatical forms in a second language, but there is a growing body of research on different types of enhancements that you can use to facilitate the acquisition of a target vocabulary.

To make vocabulary easy to understand and process, instructors might consider presenting vocabulary using pictures to clarify meaning, providing definitions of words or giving learners a list of words to familiarise themselves with ahead of time. Language instructors should ensure that vocabulary is used within a meaningful context where the input is simplified and easy to comprehend. Words can be enhanced in the input to facilitate comprehension and processing.

Once one interactive task has been set by the instructor, the question is: what kind of vocabulary do L2 learners need to complete the task? Therefore, we develop a series of sub-tasks so that we provide the necessary lexical tools for learners to complete the task. We expect learners to become familiar with relevant and useful words.

What are the main points?

A clear distinction needs to be made between mental representation and skill in language development. Language is an implicit, abstract and complex system and language development is input and input processing dependent.

Second language acquisition is constrained by certain orders and stages. Instruction might help L2 learners to develop a good level of attainment particularly if opportunities to natural exposure are given. Instruction might have a facilitative role in helping L2 learners to pay selective attention to form and form-meaning connections in the input. Although the route of acquisition cannot be altered, instruction might in certain conditions speed up the rate of acquisition. What are the conditions that might facilitate the speed in which languages are learned? A first condition is that L2 learners must be exposed to sufficient input. A second condition is that L2 learners must be developmentally ready for instruction to be effective. A third condition is that instruction must take into consideration how L2 learners process input. Traditional grammar instruction is not an appropriate way to provide L2 learners with a focus on form component in language teaching. Paradigmatic explanation of a specific linguistic form followed by mechanical drill practice is not an effective way to focus on form in the language classroom. However, there are types of 'focus on form' pedagogical interventions to grammar instruction that can, in certain cases and conditions, enhance and speed up the way languages are learned and are an effective way to incorporate grammar in language teaching. If we are going to focus on form in any way in the classroom, it ought to be input based and meaning oriented. This idea falls out of what we know about the nature of acquisition. In order to develop effective focus on form, language instructors should ensure that input is manipulated so as to facilitate language processing and acquisition. L2 learners should also be encouraged to make accurate form-meaning mappings. Language instructors must ensure they foster the development of language in L2 learners and not simply aim to foster a learning-like behaviour in L2 learners. Language instructors must use pedagogical interventions that facilitate language processing, and the development of implicit knowledge.

- There is a clear distinction to be made between focus on 'form' and focus on 'forms'. Focus on form can be described as any deliberate attempt to draw L2 learners' attention to a particular form in a meaningful context.
- Input enhancement is an input-based focus on form that might facilitate L2 learners to notice grammatical forms in the input.
- Structured input is an input-based focus on form which facilitates L2 learners to make form-meaning connections.
- Here are some of the principles that language instructors should consider when developing grammar tasks, which can provide an effective focus on form in the language classroom: (i) Grammar tasks should be developed to ensure that learners process input correctly and efficiently; (ii) Grammar tasks should be designed for learners to notice and process forms in the input and eventually make correct form-mapping connections; (iii) Grammar tasks should include both a focus on form and a focus on meaning; (iv) Grammar tasks should move from input to output practice.

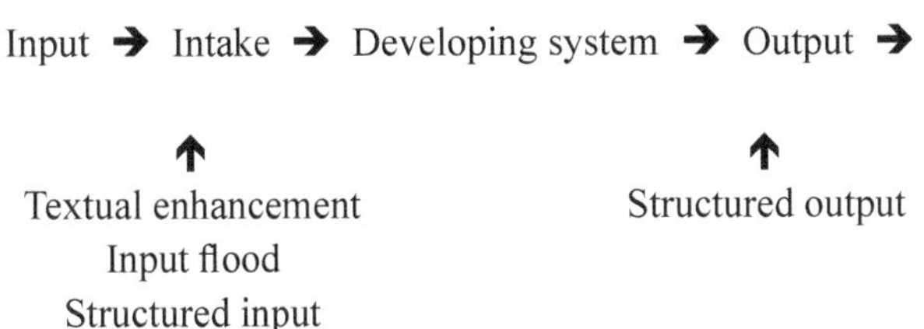

- Vocabulary instruction should keep in mind the following: present new words repeatedly and frequently in the input; use meaning-bearing comprehensible input when processing new words; present words in an enhanced manner.
- Vocabulary tasks should be input-oriented (activities or quizzes).

What else can we read?

Barcroft, J. (2018) *Vocabulary in Language Teaching.* New York: Routledge.

Benati, A. and Lee, J. (2008) *Grammar Acquisition and Processing Instruction.* Clevedon: Multilingual Matters.

Benati, A. (2021) *Focus on Form.* Cambridge: Cambridge University Press.

Benati, A. and Schwieter, J. (2019) Pedagogical interventions to L2 grammar instruction. In Schwieter, J. and Benati, A. (eds), *The Cambridge Handbook of Language Learning* (475–99). Cambridge: Cambridge University Press.

Ellis, R. (2016) Focus on form: A critical review. *Language Teaching Research*, 20: 405–28. https://doi.org/10.1177/1362168816628627

Nassaji, H. and Fotos, S. (2011) *Teaching Grammar in Second Language Classrooms*. New York: Routledge.

Lee, J. and VanPatten, B. (2003) *Making Communicative Language Teaching Happen*. New York: McGraw-Hill.

Nation, I.S.P. (2001) *Learning Vocabulary in Another Language*. Cambridge: Cambridge University Press.

Wong, W. and VanPatten, B. (2003) The Evidence in IN: Drills Are Out. *Foreign Language Annals*, 36: 403–23. https://doi.org/10.1111/j.1944-9720.2003.tb02123.x

Wong, W. (2005) *Input Enhancement: From Theory and Research to the Classroom*. New York: McGraw-Hill.

Wong, W. and Simard, D. (2018) *Focusing on Form in Language Instruction*. New York: Routledge.

6 Input

Think for a moment

One of the key questions in second language acquisition is: is input a necessary and sufficient ingredient in second language acquisition? Most theories in second language acquisition assign a key role to input. However, the lack of knowledge about the key role that comprehensible and meaningful input should play in the language classroom leads to misleading claims and misunderstanding:

- If L2 learners are not exposed to comprehensible and meaningful input, they will not process the language effectively. Learners acquire language through comprehension but they don't simply absorb everything they hear or read. They can't attach meaning to the language input they are exposed to during comprehension. This would cause a delay in acquisition of the target language.
- Simplified input is language input that is easy to process. If it is not simplified, input runs the risk of not being processed at all.
- Good input language for acquisition is not the explanation about grammar, presentation of vocabulary followed by mechanical practice. Good input language is about creating opportunities for language learners to hear or read language in a communicative context that they need to process for meaning. Explicit information about grammar rules is not input for acquisition.
- Engaging L2 learners in communication means creating opportunities for them to interpret, negotiate and express meaning in a specific context.

Language instruction should focus on providing learners with a rich variety of comprehensible input and opportunities to use language spontaneously and meaningfully. Learners' language systems process, organise, and store linguistic data continuously interacting with language input. To make its way through the system that input must be simplified input.

What is the nature and role of input?

Input refers to the language that L2 learners are exposed to (through hearing or reading) and has a communicative intent. In second language acquisition L2 learners hear or read the language that contains certain linguistic features (e.g. vocabulary, grammar, pronunciation, etc.) and other information about the L2. These features make their way into the learner's language system only if they are linked to some kind of meaning and are comprehensible to the learner. Input must be comprehensible as learners must be able to extract the meaning of the message contained in the input. Input is language that learners try to comprehend for the message contained in it.

To fully understand the nature of input it is also important to clarify what input is not. Input is meaning-oriented language that learners hear or see. It is not what they produce as what language learners produce is called output. Another important distinction to make is between input and explicit information. Explicit information (e.g. grammar explanations about the target language, to which L2 learners are often exposed in the language classroom or in textbooks) is not input for acquisition. Explicit information is not input for acquisition because in that information provided to L2 learners there is not an attempt/intention to communicate a message that learners need to attend to.

Input for acquisition is therefore the language that is embedded in a communicative context that learners attend to for its meaning. L2 learners acquire language mainly through exposure to comprehensible input, in a similar fashion to how they acquire their first language. The input that L2 learners receive should be simplified with the use of contextual and extra linguistics clues. Language learners should be exposed to comprehensible input and they should be provided with opportunities to focus on meaning rather than grammatical forms.

For the input to be effective and useful for L2 learners, it must have two main characteristics: (i) it must be comprehensible, and (ii) it must have a communicative intent. The most important thing for language acquisition to happen is that the language learner can easily understand the input. We need to ensure that the language L2 learners are exposed to is clearly and easily understood. Secondly, in order to be effective input must contain a message that learners must attend to. Learners have to be involved in an activity that has a communicative purpose. Features of language make their way to the system if they have been linked to real-world meaning.

Language is a tool for human communication, and the formal features of language – lexical items, morphology, syntax, etc. – all work together to encode meaning. So, as learners work out the meaning of the input they are exposed to, they are also making connections between the meaning of the input and the linguistic form. Several things can facilitate this process. L2 learners benefit from simplified input and modified input. Simplified input is language input that it is less complex so as to be more comprehensible. The language that native speakers (NSs) normally use to talk to young children is generally a simpler language as adults adjust their vocabulary to make the speech easier for the child to understand. In the context of L1 acquisition, children are continuously exposed to simplified input that contains a message and must be comprehended (e.g. Are you thirsty? Would you like a drink of milk? Do you like this game?). This kind of child-directed speech makes it easier for children to learn their native language. In addition, the language is highly contextualised within communicative events. What this means is that children at the age of two, for example, are hearing language that is embedded in concrete, here-and-now situations – even during storytelling when they are looking at pictures.

In the second language acquisition context, we also find that simplified input is effective. Evelyn Hatch noted that simplified input to L2 learners consists of a variety of characteristics when compared to native-to-native speech: slower speech rate (and thus clearer articulation), use of high-frequency vocabulary, pausing at appropriate places with pauses often longer and more frequent, rephrasing, and the use of shorter and simpler sentences.

The use of shorter sentences, for example, reduces the information-processing burden on the L2 learner. Additional pausing does the same thing: pauses give learners 'processing time' before the next round of information comes in. These modifications result in greater likelihood of comprehension, which in turn facilitates the conditions for acquisition.

Michael Long investigated how the structure of an interaction can be modified to make input more comprehensible for non-native speakers (NNSs). Through these interactions, L2 learners have the advantage of being able to negotiate meaning and make some conversational adjustments. Negotiation of meaning refers to the efforts made by both NSs and NNSs to modify the interaction in order to ensure comprehension along the lines of what Evelyn Hatch has described. Learners sometimes request clarifications or repetitions if they do not understand the input they receive. In short, negotiation of meaning leads to input modification by the other speaker, and this leads to greater overall comprehension for the L2 learner. When learners comprehend more, they 'process' more of the input and this facilitates second language acquisition.

Rhonda Oliver has identified three of the most common types of interactional modifications to negotiate meaning: comprehension checks; confirmation checks; and clarification requests. Comprehension checks are used when one speaker is not convinced that the other speaker has understood what has been said (e.g. *Do you understand? Do you follow me?*). Clarification requests are expressions used to clarify speakers' utterances (e.g. *What did you say? Huh?*). Confirmation checks are used to ensure that one speaker has clearly understood what said by another speaker (e.g. Is this what you mean?). These types of interactions provide L2 learners with comprehensible input and opportunities for acquisition.

L2 learners are exposed to a vast amount of input. However, not all the input L2 learners are exposed to is actually processed. Pit Corder made an important distinction between input and intake. Input refers to what is available to the learner, and intake is the part of the input actually internalised by the language learner. Intake is the portion of the input that is 'taken in' by the learner. It is often the case that when acquiring another language we are exposed to language that is totally incomprehensible (e.g. the announcements made at train stations, where the language is fast and sometimes unclear). Learners don't understand the input and therefore that input is not integrated into the current learner language acquisition system. In order for that input to make its way into the language internal system it must first be comprehensible. Despite this important feature, it is not possible for learners to take in all the input they are exposed to as humans have limited capacity to process and store information. There are a number of positions/theoretical views about the fact that for input to be usable for acquisition it must be attended and noticed in some ways.

Richard Schmidt has argued that L2 learners require attention in order to successfully process forms in the input. Learners must pay attention to a form in the input and notice that form for that form to be acquired. A degree of awareness is also crucial for L2 learners to incorporate the new language into their internal system. However, for Russell Tomlin and Victor Villa input must be detected, and this process does not involve awareness. Whether or not awareness plays a role, input must be noticed. L2 learners must pay attention to the input language they are exposed to. Bill VanPatten assigns a crucial role to input and argues that language acquisition happens as a by-product of language comprehension. His model of input processing focuses on what learners process and don't process in the input and why. He argues that when L2 learners attend to or notice input to comprehend a message a form-meaning connection is made. When learners process input, they filter the input, which is reduced and modified into a new entity (intake). Only part of the input L2 learners receive is processed and becomes intake. This is mainly due to processing limitations (memory capacity) and processing strategies. Bill VanPatten has identified a series of processing strategies used by L2 learners when they process and filter linguistic data at the level of input. These strategies/principles allow learners to selectively attend to incoming stimuli without being overloaded with information.

During language input processing, L2 learners initially direct their attention towards the detection of content words to understand the meaning of an utterance. Learners tend to focus their attention on content words in order to understand the message of the input they are exposed to. In doing so, they do not process grammatical forms, and consequently they fail to make form-meaning connections. This is the case for forms which are redundant in the input for example. Redundancy is when, in a sentence or discourse, both a grammatical form and a word encode the same semantic information. For example, when learners try to make moment-by-moment connections between surface forms and meaning for the sentence *Yesterday, I played tennis with John in the park*, they need to tag *played* as a verb (<+V>, <-N>), that its meaning refers to playing a sport, that it is past tense not present (<+present> <-past>), and so on. However, because learners process the first element (the lexical item *Yesterday*) before they encounter the verb, they already know to interpret the sentence as a past time event. Thus, they can skip the form *-ed* in *played* as it encodes the same semantic information. The presence of a lexical item encoding the same referential meaning as the linguistic form makes the form redundant in this sentence and prevents learners from making an immediate form-meaning connection.

L2 learners also tend to process the first noun or pronoun they encounter in a sentence as the subject or agent. This processing strategy leads them to misinterpret the meaning of an utterance and may cause delays in acquisition. L2 learners must be able to determine which is the subject and which is the object in a sentence they hear or read. Linked to this processing principle is the concept of parsing. One of the main functions of parsing is to figure out who did what to whom in a sentence. In the sentence *The police officer was killed by the robber*, learners, in an attempt to make moment-by-moment computation of sentence structure during comprehension, would process the first element they encounter in the sentence as the subject of the sentence. So, L2 learners would interpret the sentence as if it were the police officer who killed the robber. This will cause a delay in interpreting the meaning of the sentence and therefore a subsequent delay in the acquisition of syntactic structures that don't follow the expected word order, such as passive constructions, causative forms.

Brian MacWhinney has pointed out that all linguistic performance requires making connections between language forms and functions. The forms are morphological inflections and word order patterns. The functions are grammatical functions with specific semantic properties. The mapping of one form and one function is part of first language (L1) acquisition, and, according to this model, second language acquisition involves adjusting the existing mapping system in the L1 acquisition so that it is appropriate for the second language system.

Within this framework, input plays a key role in terms of providing multiple cues for the learners. According to this model, the acquisition of appropriate form-meaning mappings is driven by a number of factors mainly related to how reliable a particular cue is. One main factor contributing to the reliability of a given cue is frequency. This factor relates to how often a form-meaning connection occurs in the input. If it is frequent, then the cue is strengthened and L2 learners can rely on the particular cue.

Second language acquisition is intake dependent since only input that has been noticed and processed is usable for acquisition. Exposure to input is both necessary and sufficient for child L1 learners to acquire all the components of their native language. In other words, without input, children will not learn the L1. At the same time, access to input is the only thing that children need to learn the L1. The question for L2 learners is whether input is also both a necessary and sufficient condition for L2 acquisition. All L2 researchers agree that L2 acquisition will not happen without access to input. They disagree, however, on whether input is the only thing learners need. The debate is around whether output and interaction also play central roles in L2 development. Because L2 learners have a wider variety of outcomes than L1 learners, some researchers believe that input alone is not enough for L2 learners to acquire a second language. Other researchers have pointed out that a key difference between L1 and L2 acquisition is that L1 learners are exposed to a richer variety and different quality of input in comparison to learners learning an L2 in a foreign-language learning context. Indeed, there is evidence that quantity and quality of input matter for L2 learners. L2 learners who are immersed in the target language, either because they live in the country where the language is spoken or because they are studying subjects such as business or arts via the target second language, have access to more and better input than students in traditional foreign language classes. Findings from immersion studies clearly indicate that immersion-language learning is superior to the foreign-language learning experience. Learners are exposed to a higher quantity of input and a better quality as the input learners are exposed to communicative input. This is also the case of the study-abroad experience. Learners who develop advanced proficiency in an L2 usually have some immersion experience.

Input is a necessary and vital factor for second language acquisition as it provides the primary linguistic data for the creation of an implicit unconscious linguistic system. Perspectives may differ as to what happens to the input as the learner interacts with it and what winds up in the head but they all concur that the data for language acquisition are in the input.

Morgan-Short has outlined that empirical research from neurolinguistic studies that provide learners with meaningful L2 input alone indicate that input may be sufficient to bring about some level of learning and language-related neural processing. Comprehension of input is critical for acquisition, and we should study it moment-by-moment as it proceeds. What is needed, then, is research on how mental representation develops as a result of language processing. Online (real-time) measurements are less susceptible to the use of explicit knowledge than offline (untimed) measurements for example. Under time pressure, L2 learners do not have time to access and apply their explicitly learned knowledge.

What are the main points?

Although exposure to input is necessary and vital for second language acquisition, mere exposure to input might not be sufficient and sometimes input might need to be enhanced via some kind of formal instruction. Input can be enhanced so as to increase the possibility that L2 learners might notice particular forms in the input they are exposed to. Textual enhancement is an instructional intervention carried out to enhance the saliency of input in written or oral texts with a view to facilitating learners' noticing of targeted forms and thereby enhancing their acquisition. Textual enhancement makes use of typographical cues (e.g. boldfacing, italicising, underlining, colouring, enlarging the font size, etc.) to draw learners' attention to particular forms in a text. Overall, research on input and textual enhancement has indicated that it is an effective input manipulation pedagogical intervention to increase frequency about a target form in the input and foster noticing (see Chapter 7 in this book).

Input can be restructured so that form-meaning connections can be facilitated. Processing instruction is a pedagogical intervention to grammar instruction that exposes L2 learners to a particular type of input to push learners away from non-optimal processing strategies mentioned earlier so that they are more likely to make correct form-meaning connections or parse sentences appropriately (compute basic structure in real time) during comprehension. Processing instruction relies on structured input tasks to push learners away from inefficient processing strategies so that they are more likely to process the relevant forms in the input. Overall, the research into the effects of Processing Instruction on the interpretation and processing of target structures has revealed that it is an effective input-based pedagogical intervention.

Interactional input refers to input received during interaction where there is some kind of communicative exchange involving the learner and at least one other person (e.g. conversation, classroom interactions). In these exchanges, L2 learners negotiate meaning and make some conversational adjustments. This means that conversation and interaction may make linguistic features salient to the learner and the process of negotiating meaning can facilitate acquisition. Learners sometimes request clarifications or repetitions if they do not understand the input they receive. In the attempt to facilitate communication, one person can request the other to modify his/

her utterances or the person modifies their own utterances to be understood. This kind of negotiation of meaning may trigger interactional adjustments by the NS or more competent interlocutor. Negotiation of meaning may facilitate language acquisition because it connects input, learner-internal capacities, particularly selective attention, and output in productive ways. Research into the relative effectiveness of modified input on acquisition has shown it might have an impact on learners' ability to negotiate the input they need at a particular stage of development.

Corrective feedback can provide learners with additional input and indicate that utterances are not target-like. This can take several forms in conversational interaction, such as puzzled looks, confirmation checks, clarifications requests, and corrective recasts. Recast is where learners are provided with a correct form in the input. The interlocutor will reformulate a learner's non-target-like utterance so that it is target-like in the hopes that the learner becomes aware that something is wrong in their output. Research on the effects of recasts has provided mixed results. Some researchers have argued that corrective feedback is more effective when L2 learners are actively engaged in negotiating a form, or when they have to think about and respond to the other speaker's feedback in some way.

What is input in the context of acquiring languages? Input is the language that L2 learners hear or see in a communicative context. Input is language that learners try to comprehend for the message contained in it. When somebody says '*Di Dove sei?* (Where are you from?) I focus on what (input) the person is asking me/would like to know and my answer will be *Sono di Milano* (I am from Milan). I am responding, focusing on the meaning contained in what this person is saying/asking me.

In contrast I can hear my teacher asking me and/or the entire classroom to repeat something or explaining something (e.g. grammatical feature). My task would simply be to repeat or memorise some language.

It would certainly be the case that I can repeat without knowing what my teacher is actually saying. I could perform the activity without fully understanding the meaning.

It is important to reiterate here that input for acquisition is the language that is embedded in a communicative context that learners attend to for its meaning. L2 learners acquire language mainly through exposure to comprehensible input, in a similar fashion to how they acquire their first language. The input that L2 learners receive should therefore be simplified with the use of contextual and extra linguistics clues. Language learners should be provided with opportunities to focus on meaning rather than grammatical forms for example.

Simplified input is language input that is easy to process. Teachers can, for example, use high-frequency vocabulary. They can also make use of gestures, pictures or drawings to make input simpler and easier to comprehend. The use of short sentences can also reduce the burden of processing and increase comprehension.

Good input language for learning is not an explanation of grammar, or a presentation of vocabulary followed by mechanical practice. Good input language is about creating opportunities for language learners to hear or read language in a communicative context that they need to process for meaning. Engaging language learners in communication means to creating opportunities for them to interpret, negotiate and express meaning in a specific context. Language teaching should focus on providing learners with a rich variety of comprehensible input and opportunities to use language spontaneously and meaningfully. Interaction offers opportunities for negotiation of meaning and language acquisition. Quality classroom input must have two characteristics:

(a) It needs to be at an appropriate level.
(b) Learners should be engaged with the input (they interact with it).

Learners acquire language through comprehension but they don't simply absorb everything they hear or read. They can't attach meaning to the language input they are exposed to during comprehension.

Their language systems process, organise, and store linguistic data continuously interacting with language input. To make its way through the system, that input must be simplified input (see examples below).

NS: Hello, my name is Alessandro. What is your name?
NNS: [pause]
NS: What is your name? Are you Robert? Paul? What is your name?
NNS: Oh, uh, Frank.
NS: Thanks. (To somebody else): Hello. My name is Alessandro. What is your name?
NNS: Uh, Grace.

NS: Right. (To all the class): We have two students. He is Frank and
    she is Grace.
    And you, what is your name?
NNS: Alex.
NS: Are you Alex?
NNS: [nodding]
NS: (to all the class): He is Alex. And you, what is your name?

There are five features in the above exchanges which should be considered
to make input language easy to understand and process.

- Short sentences
- Repetition
- Slower rate
- Rephrasing
- Content is clear.

The instructor is focused on getting everyone's name out so that learners
can know each other. Learners are mapping overall meaning into strings
of words they hear or read. The content is clear as instructors use linguistic and non-linguistic means to make input comprehensible (pictures,
cartoons, gestures). As the level of language improves and learners make
steady progress, instructors naturally shift the input to be of an appropriate level.

Takeaways

To recap, the main takeaways are:

- Input matters in second language acquisition as it plays an es-
  sential role.
- Input should be central to the classroom, not something added on.
- Input must be simplified, comprehensible, and level-appropriate
- Input must be message-oriented.
- Instructors should be talking with L2 learners and not at learners.

What else can we read?

Ellis, N.C. (2012) Frequency-based accounts of SLA. In Gass, S.M. and Mackey, A. (eds), *Handbook of Second Language Acquisition* (193–210). New York: Routledge.

Gass, S. M. and Mackey, A. (2015) Input, interaction and output in second language acquisition. In VanPatten, B. and Williams, J. (eds), *Theories in Second Language Acquisition* (2nd edn) (180–206). New York: Routledge.

Hatch, E.M. (1983) Simplified input and second language acquisition. In Andersen, R.W. (ed.), *Pidginization and Creolization as Language Acquisition* (64–86). Cambridge, MA: Newbury House.

Krashen, S. (1982) *Second Language Acquisition and Second Language Learning*. Oxford: Pergamon.

Krashen, S. (2009) The comprehension hypothesis extended. In Piske, T. and Young-Scholten, M. (eds), *Input Matters* (81–94). Bristol: Multilingual Matters.

Lichtman, K., VanPatten, B. (2021) Was Krashen right? Forty years later. *Foreign Language Annals*, 54(2): 283–305. https://doi.org/10.1111/flan.12552

Long, M.H. (1985) Input and second language acquisition theory. In Gass, S. M. and Madden, C. G. (eds), *Input in Second Language Acquisition* (377–93). Rowley, MA: Newbury House.

MacWhinney, B. (1987) The competition model. In MacWhinney, B. (ed), *Mechanism of Language Acquisition* (249–308). Hillsdale, NJ: Lawrence Erlbaum Associates.

Morgan-Short, K. (2021) Considering the updated Input Hypothesis from a neurolinguistic perspective: A response to Lichtman and VanPatten. *Foreign Language Annals*, 54(2): 324–30. https://doi.org/10.1111/flan.12551

VanPatten, B. (2004) On the role(s) of input and output in making form-meaning connections. In VanPatten, B., Williams, J., Rott, S. and Overstreet, M. (eds), *Form-meaning Connections in Second Language Acquisition* (29–47). Mahwah, NJ: Lawrence Erlbaum Associates.

VanPatten, B. (2015) Input processing in adult SLA. In VanPatten, B. and Williams, J. (eds), *Theories in Second Language Acquisition* (2nd edn) (113–35). New York: Routledge.

7 Instruction

Can we take a minute to think about this?

What is the of role of instruction is a key question in second language acquisition and second language teaching. and a central issue in the field of SLA. Does language practice make a difference? For instruction we refer to any explicit or implicit interventions to draw L2 learners' attention to formal properties of a second language. Very often the misleading answer to this question is that practice enhances language acquisition. The truth of the matter is that instruction has a very limited role in second language acquisition.

Empirical research conducted in the last thirty years has focused on measuring the role of instruction in affecting the route (learning of various features in a specific order); the rate (learning of features at a specific speed); and the ultimate level of second language attainment (reaching higher or lower proficiency levels). Scholars have provided us with a succinct review of the role of instruction in second language acquisition. Overall, they have identified two main views around the role of instruction:

(i)   The first view is that instruction has a limited and constrained role.
(ii) The second view is that instruction could have a beneficial role under certain conditions. First, it might bring L2 learners' attention to things in the input that might not be appropriately processed (e.g. making correct form-meaning connections). Second, the language classroom can provide L2 learners with a rich and complex input.

What is the nature and role of instruction?

Second language acquisition theory argues that instruction plays a limited role in second language acquisition. Acquisition is an unconscious and implicit process, and L2 learners acquire a second language through exposure to comprehensible and meaningful input rather than learning grammar consciously through explicit grammatical rules. In addition to the limited role assigned to grammar instruction, it is also argued that L2 learners acquired grammatical features (e.g. morphemes) of a target language in a predictable order and this is regardless of their first language or the context in which they acquire them. In the English language, for example, progressive -ing is acquired before regular past tense -ed, which is acquired before third-person -s. Instruction might be unable to alter the route of acquisition as L2 learners follow specific orders of acquisition.

In addition to order of acquisition, L2 learners acquire single structures through predictable stages. In fact, instruction is constrained by these developmental stages, and L2 learners follow a very rigid route in the acquisition of grammatical features which cannot be skipped. If instruction is targeted to grammatical features for which L2 learners are developmentally ready, then instruction can be beneficial in helping them to move faster along their natural route of development. Each language feature actually has stages of acquisition.

However, instruction might help L2 learners to develop a good level of attainment particularly if opportunities to natural exposure are given. It might have a facilitative role when it is used for linguistic features, which are not too distant from the learner's current level of language development. It might have a facilitative role in helping L2 learners to pay selective attention to form and form-meaning connections in the input. Learners make form-meaning connections from the input they receive as they connect particular meanings to particular forms (grammatical or lexical). Therefore, learners must be trained on how to process input more effectively and efficiently so that they are in a better position to process grammatical forms and connect them with their meanings. We therefore suggest the phrase 'manipulation of input' rather than the word 'instruction'. Does manipulating input make a difference?

The beneficial role that instruction might play in second language acquisition is based on the assumption that the route of acquisition cannot be altered. However, instruction might in certain conditions speed up the rate of acquisition and the development of greater language proficiency.

What are the conditions that might facilitate the speed in which languages are learned?

- A first condition is that L2 learners must be exposed to sufficient input.
- A second condition is that L2 learners must be psycholinguistically ready for instruction to be effective as indicated by Pienemann.
- A third condition is that instruction must take into consideration how L2 learners process input.

What are the main points?

Considering that language is complex, implicit and abstract, language instruction should not consist of explanation of rules and mechanical practice. Traditional instruction might help to develop a language-like behaviour (skill) but is not responsible for language development (mental representation of language). A basic review of the empirical evidence suggests:

- Instruction might help L2 learners to develop a good level of attainment particularly if opportunities for natural exposure to language input are given. Instruction has a facilitative role when it is used for linguistic features, which are not too distant from the learner's current level of language development.
- Instruction might have a facilitative role in helping learners to pay selective attention to form and form-meaning connections in the input. Learners make form-meaning connections from the input they receive as they connect particular meanings to particular forms (grammatical or lexical). For example, they tend to connect a form with its meaning in the input they receive (the morpheme -*ed* on the end of a verb in English refers to an event in the past).
- Instruction should move from input to output practice. Initially, input-based and interactional options to instruction might help L2 learners to internalise the grammatical features of a target language.
- Overall, the role of instruction in language acquisition is limited and constrained by a number of factors (e.g. orders and sequences of development, processing constraints). However, despite the fact that instruction is, for instance, not able to alter the route of acquisition, it might have some beneficial effects in terms of speeding up the rate of language acquisition. The question is how.

> If we are going to focus on form in any way in the classroom, it ought to be input based and meaning oriented. Instruction as input manipulation might or might not facilitate language processing.

Instruction should be less about the teaching of rules and more about exposure to form. Input (comprehensible and meaningful) is an indispensable element in language development. Instruction ought to be less about manipulating output and more about processing input (input manipulations through input enhancement and structured input). Although output is constraint by processability, meaningful output practice has a role in language development. Future research needs to be appropriate and sound empirical research making use of psycholinguistic and neuro-linguistic methodological tools to further investigate the role and nature of language instruction. Future language instructor training programs must fully consider the role and nature of language and language development and provide language instructors with a more evidence and principle-based approach to language instruction.

What else can we read?

Krashen, S. (1982) *Second Language Acquisition and Second Language Learning*. Oxford, Pergamon.

Gass, S. (2003) Input and interaction. In Doughty, C. and Long, M. (eds), *The Handbook of Second Language Acquisition* (224–55). Oxford: Blackwell.

Long, M. (1996) The role of the linguistic environment in second language acquisition. In Ritchie W., and Bhatia T. (eds), *Handbook of Second Language Acquisition* (413–68). San Diego, CA: Academic Press.

8   Interaction and Negotiation of Meaning

Can we take a minute to think about this?

Interacting with both native speakers and non-native speakers might facilitate exposure to input and comprehension of language which consequently enhances language acquisition. There is overall agreement among second language researchers that input is indispensable for acquisition. However, the lack of knowledge about what is the actual role and effects of interaction and negotiation of meaning might lead to some misunderstandings and misleading claims:

- Second language researchers seem to agree that output, especially as part of interaction, may enhance the acquisition of lexical items and their meanings. However, there is no empirical evidence showing that output and interaction facilitate the acquisition of syntax and there is also no evidence that output and interaction might play any significant role in the properties of language governed by universal grammar.
- There is a link between output and interaction for the developing of language skills, however, there is *no link* between these two constructs and the development of competence and/or language as mental representation.
- There is tendency to use oral practice which is traditional and does not take into consideration the best way to engage L2 learners in interaction and negotiation of meaning.
- In traditional oral practice, L2 learners would be asked to talk about a specific topic 'How do you spend your free time and over the weekend?' In this kind of exercise (open-ended question) L2 learners will have very little time to talk and no opportunities to interact meaningfully.

What is the nature and role of interaction and negotiation of meaning?

The main view is that interactions might affect acquisition with the understanding that input is a key ingredient for the acquisition of a second language. Interactional input refers to input received during interaction where there is some kind of communicative exchange involving the learner and at least one other person. Interactions might enhance comprehension which in turn might affect acquisition in essentially two ways: (1) by modifying input; and (2) by providing feedback related to the linking of meaning and form. Through these interactions, L2 learners have the advantage of being able to negotiate meaning and make some conversational adjustments. Input modifications happen when the other speaker adjusts his or her speech due to perceived difficulties in learner comprehension or to provide corrective feedback. Two reasonable claims can be made about the nature of input, interaction and negotiation of meaning:

- Input is an essential element in language acquisition. It consists of two types: interactional and non-interactional. Interactional input is the one received during interaction where there is some kind of communicative exchange involving the learner and at least another person (e.g. conversation, classroom interactions, etc.); non-interactional input occurs in the context of non-reciprocal discourse and learners are not part of an interaction (e.g. announcements).
- Interaction might play an important role in second language acquisition in certain circumstances. Language modifications can help lead L2 learners to notice things they wouldn't be noticed otherwise, and the noticing of certain linguistic features in the input is an important step in initially processing language. However, for language processing to take place more effectively and to have an impact on language acquisition, form-meaning mappings need to take place.
- Negotiation of meaning in conversations or interactions refers to a communication breakdown between two speakers and where an adjustment is made to facilitate comprehension; corrective feedback is used when a speaker indicates to another speaker that what he/she has produced is non-native-like. Interactions that elicit feedback can have a facilitative role in acquisition. Through ap-

propriate interactions, L2 learners have the advantage of being able to negotiate meaning and make some conversational adjustments. Negotiation of meaning refers to the efforts made by both NSs and NNSs to modify the interaction in order to ensure comprehension. L2 learners sometimes request clarifications or repetitions if they do not understand the input they receive. In short, negotiation of meaning leads to input modification by the other speaker, and this leads to greater overall comprehension for the L2 learner. When learners comprehend more, they 'process' more of the input and this facilitates second language acquisition. Three of the most common types of interactional modifications to negotiate meaning are:

(i)   Comprehension checks; confirmation checks; and clarification requests. Comprehension checks are used when one speaker is not convinced that the other speaker has understood what has been said (e.g. *Do you understand? Do you follow me?*);

(ii) Clarification requests are expressions used to clarify speakers' utterances (e.g. *What did you say? Huh?*).

(iii) Confirmation checks are used to ensure that one speaker has clearly understood what is said by another speaker (e.g. *Is this what you mean?*). These types of interactions provide L2 learners with comprehensible input and opportunities for acquisition.

Classroom-based research investigating the effects of groups and learner-to-learner interaction and negotiation of meaning has overall provided the following consistent findings:

- L2 learners have more opportunities to use the target language.
- L2 learners have more opportunities to use the language communicatively (clarifications, confirmation and comprehension checks).
- L2 learners perform better.

Classroom-based research into the relative effectiveness of modified input on acquisition has shown it might have an impact on learners' ability to negotiate the input they need at a particular stage of development.

- L2 learners should have the opportunity to control the topic of conversation and to self-initiate.
- L2 language instructors and L2 learners must negotiate meaning.
- L2 learners must be challenged to operate beyond their current level of competence.
- L2 learners must have the opportunity to participate in planned and unplanned discourse.
- L2 language instructors should provide sufficient models of discourse containing many samples of linguistic features that learners are trying to learn.

Assuming that our aim is to develop L2 learners' communicative competence, we must create classroom oral tasks that stimulate interaction and negotiation of meaning opportunities in the language classroom. Classroom discussion must not be dominated by a minority of talkative participants and all L2 learners must contribute equally. In traditional oral practice, language instructors and L2 learners normally exchange very little real information. Language instructors spend most of their time asking 'displayed questions' for which learners already know the answers. Typically, an instructor asks a question (e.g. Where is the pen? Showing everybody that the pen is on the table) for which he/she and the learners know the answer, an individual learner answers, the instructor evaluates or corrects the answer, and then the cycle begins again with another learner and another question to which everyone already knows the answer. Display questions have clear limitations as, on one hand, they do not offer genuine communication practice, and on the other hand, they take learners away from the use of language for communicative purposes. The question is: how do we provide a better approach to offer opportunities to exchange real information through interaction and negotiation of meaning? Here are some suggestions:

- Language instructors should increase L2 learners' talk time and at the same time lowers the inhibitions of L2 learners who are unwilling to speak in front of the full class. In group work, L2 learners perform a learning task through small-group interaction. One of the advantages is that it can foster learner responsibility and independence.
- Language instructors should use easy and comprehensible language that will help L2 learners to interact with language.

- Language instructors should use target language in the language classroom.
- L2 learners should be allowed to initiate communication, and classroom language tasks should involve negotiation for meaning.
- Language instructors should provide positive feedback on learners' speech.
- Language instructors should choose an interesting and familiar topic for interaction which enables L2 learners to use ideas from their own experience and knowledge.
- Language instructors should provide clear opportunities for interaction through pair-group work. They need to make sure that everyone in the group contributes to the discussion by appointing a chairperson to each group who will regulate participation. They need to create a classroom environment where L2 learners are exposed to real-life communication.
- Language instructors should encourage goal-oriented activities that require the group or pair achieve an objective that is usually expressed by an observable result, such as brief notes or lists, a rearrangement of jumbled items, a drawing, a spoken summary. This should be attainable only by interaction between participants.

The role of the language instructors must be of the one of 'a resource person' and 'architect' as they structure the conversation but they are not responsible for its final accomplishment. L2 learners must take initiative and responsibility to complete the task. They need to take the initiative and make decisions in order to complete a language task successfully. This can occur when students collaborate in groups to achieve a goal or to complete a task. L2 learners must be given a task where they need something to talk about and someone to talk to.

What are the main points?

Although exposure to input is necessary and vital for second language acquisition, mere exposure to input might not be sufficient, and sometimes input might need to be enhanced via some kind of formal instruction. Interactional input refers to input received during interaction where there is some kind of communicative exchange involving the learner and at least one other person (e.g. conversation, classroom interactions). L2 learners must develop their ability to manage interaction as well as engage in the negotiation of meaning.

The management of the interaction involves such things as when and how to take the floor, when to introduce a topic or change the subject, how to invite someone else to speak, how to keep a conversation going and so on. In these exchanges, L2 learners negotiate meaning and make some conversational adjustments. This means that conversation and interaction may make linguistic features salient to the learner and the process of negotiating meaning can facilitate acquisition.

L2 learners sometimes request clarifications or repetitions if they do not understand the input they receive. In the attempt to facilitate communication, one person can request the other to modify his/her utterances, or the person modifies their own utterances to be understood. This kind of negotiation of meaning may trigger interactional adjustments by the NS or more competent interlocutor. Negotiation of meaning may facilitate language acquisition because it connects input, learner-internal capacities, particularly selective attention, and output in productive ways.

Language instructors must use the target language at all times in the classroom interaction. By doing this they are providing input for acquisition. Developing an interactive activity facilitates comprehension and communication in the language classroom. Based on what has been presented and examined here, some practical suggestions for language teaching are provided:

- Language instructors and L2 learners should interact with each other in a language task. The role of the instructor is as the one who designs the task and encourages participation and contribution from L2 learners. The learner's role is to share responsibility in interaction and task completion. By providing a series of tasks to complete we encourage learners to take responsibility for generating the information themselves rather than just receiving it.
- Language instructors should reduce their speaking time in class and increase learners' speaking time.
- Language instructors should ask eliciting questions in order to prompt L2 learners to interact with NS and NNS.
- Language instructors should give learners positive feedback. They should indicate positive signs when interacting.

- Language instructors should provide L2 learners with a rich environment where meaningful communication takes place.

What else can we read?

Bygate, M (1987) *Speaking*. Oxford: Oxford University Press.

Ellis, R. (2003) *Task-based Language Learning and Teaching*. Oxford: Oxford University Press.

Lee, J. (2000) *Tasks and Communicating in Language Classrooms*. New York: McGraw-Hill.

Lee, J. and VanPatten, B. (2003) *Making Communicative Language Teaching Happen*. New York: McGraw-Hill.

Littlewood, W. (1981) *Communicative Language Teaching. An Introduction*. Oxford: Oxford University Press.

Savignon, S. (2005) *Communicative Competence. Theory and Classroom Practice*. New York: McGraw-Hill.

9   Language

(with Víctor Parra-Guinaldo)

Can we take a minute to think about this?

Language teacher training programs aim at ensuring that experienced teachers and/or trainees develop a good understanding of how principles derived from theory and research can be applied in day-to-day language teaching. These programs are often module-based and cover a number of areas and issues: from how to teach grammar, to how to develop language skills through classroom practice. One of their limitations is that they neither include a module on 'language' nor discuss the real nature of language. The lack of knowledge about what language is and how it works leads to misleading claims and misunderstanding:

- The first consequence is the perpetuation of the myth that what it is on page 33 of a language textbook (e.g. explanation of rules, paradigms) is what winds up in our head. Such a myth includes the idea that language is a list of rules, such as those found in text-books, or that such things as verbal paradigms are psychologically real in the sense that expert speakers and knowers of a language actually have paradigms in their heads (we don't!). Paradigms are often used by textbook authors to summarise grammatical points or specific language structures. Although they might provide a useful summary for language learners, they don't correspond to the way that grammar is processed in our mind/brain.
- The second consequence is the perpetuation of traditional approaches to language teaching (e.g. Grammar Translation Method, Audio-lingual Method). Teachers and instructors believe that what it is on that page 33 is a representation of what language is and how it works. However, what winds up in our head is different and there is no mechanism in the brain which can turn explicit knowledge into implicit knowledge.

- The third consequence is the inability to convince colleagues and administrators about the real nature of language. The idea that language is what we see in textbooks, and can be taught in a traditional sense is engrained in their heads. Teacher education, very often, tends to perpetuate these ideas and this has an impact on how we evaluate language learning and language proficiency through a specific set of tests and grades.
- The fourth consequence is that much empirical research in the field of instructed second language acquisition focuses on the learning of what we see in textbooks. This research generally leads to misconceptions and misleading statements about the nature and the acquisition of languages.

The question is: How do we arrive at an accurate and workable definition of language?

What is the nature and role of language?

First of all, let's define what language is not. Language is not subject-matter in the typical or traditional sense. Languages are not learned in the same way we learn history, English literature and any other disciplines. In fact, language is not something to be learned the way a person learns anything else (e.g. playing tennis, driving a car, playing cards, etc.). Practice does not make perfect! Language is a complex, abstract, constrained and implicit system. Let's examine these four attributes in turn.

Complex

Language can be described as multi-componential and a complex system. Learning a language means acquiring a number of elements:

- The total stock of words (lexicon), or signs in the case of sign languages, word elements and their meanings.
- The sounds (phonology) that make up words (pronunciation) or hand gestures (visual cues), and the way they come together to form speech, words, or gestures in the case of sign language.

- The patterns (morphology) of word formation (e.g. inflections on verbs and nouns), or sign combinations, and how new words are made from other words (e.g. prefixes and suffixes).
- The rules of sentence structure (syntax) to explain what combination of words or signs is permissible or not in a language.
- The use of sentences to intend something specific (pragmatics). The role of context in language and how people rely on it for successful communication.
- The study of language and how it functions in society (sociolinguistics). The study of the interaction between linguistic and social variables, such as when it is appropriate to use different types of language.
- The way sentences or sequences of signs are connected (discourse). How coherent and cohesive linguistic elements are in sentences.

Learning a language means acquiring all these elements all at the same time. Each person, no matter whether it is a first, second or third language, creates an internal language system we call language. This system is abstract in nature as its features are difficult to describe with exact words. What we observe as 'language' is the result of a complex interaction of principles, constraints, and interfaces that yield utterances (just few examples below).

Language is constrained by the quantity and quality of input. The formal environment (language classroom) tends not to offer the same kind and amount of input as the outside world. The context may constrain acquisition because it constrains access to the amount and type of input learners get.

Language is constrained by developmental sequences. The way that learners can string together elements to produce a sentence is constrained by internal processing procedures which follow a predictable order (e.g. we have access to the use of single words before more complex syntactic structures to string elements of the language together in a sentence). For example, in the use of English negation, language learners first access the simple No + X = *No drink* before subject and negation move inside the sentence = *I don't drink*).

Abstract and constrained

This abstract language representation bears no resemblance to rules found in language textbooks. Much of the grammatical information is stored in lexical entries with embedded features (see examples below).

e.g. *Does* [<Q>, <T> <+V> <-V> + <present > <-past> 3rd person sing].

Does, for example stores the feature <Q> (Question) and <+V> (Verb) and encodes the temporal meaning <present> and someone else is doing the action. This complex and abstract system is also implicit as we know we have language in our heads, but we don't really know what the contents are.

Basic constructs in language are largely indefinable in everyday terms. For example, what is a verb? A verb in any language can represent a variety of concepts such as actions (e.g. to run), states (e.g. to remain), experiences (e.g. to like). However, what kind of verb is rain? It is not an action, or any of the other categories, so what is it? What makes states verb different from adjectives? Tired, happy, dead, restful, are all adjectives representing 'states'. In the sentence *I am tired* what is the verb and can we describe it? The suffix *-ing* is used to make one of the inflected forms of English verbs. This suffix is added to the stem of the verb to express that an action is not completed (progressive). This definition works for the first example (a) but it does not work for the second (b).

(a)   John is eating
(b)   John is being happy.

From all these examples, the point is that the most basic things we rely on to talk about language are too abstract to define in everyday terms.

There are many aspects of language that are universal and built in prior to exposure to the input language. We have an innate knowledge of what is allowed and what is disallowed in a language. This is what we call 'grammaticality judgment'. For example, first language speakers of English know (without being taught) the following:

(a)   *I've done it* (contraction of *I have* is allowed)
(b)   *Should I've done it?* (contraction here is disallowed)

How does a person come to know that *I've* (and contractions more generally) is allowed in some instances and disallowed in others? No one teaches a child! And yet every native speaker of English comes to know what is disallowed with contractions. This is what we call a universal feature that is available to humans from the start!

Language is composed of abstract principles. One such principle is the Structure-Dependence Principle, which states that 'All syntactic operations are structure dependent.' What this means is that language learners don't apply syntactic (grammatical) operations on a specific word or on a particular word order; instead, these operations occur at the phrase level, where these words are contained in a hierarchical fashion. Therefore, it is the phrases that are the foci of syntactic operations. For example, if a language learner hears in English, *John will come tomorrow* and *Will John come tomorrow?* that learner could assume that yes/no questions are formed by either (1) moving the second word to the front or (2) by simple subject–verb inversion. This assumption would lead to errors such as the following: *Eats John chocolate?* from *John eats chocolate.* Such error does not occur in either first or second language acquisition. This is because the Structure-Dependence Principle requires that operations happen on phrases and not individual words. A modal, such as *will*, is interpreted as an element located in a different part of the phrase to the main verb, since these are different types of verb and they behave differently within the phrase. Thus, learners inherently 'know' certain things about what languages can and cannot do, and these things are the universal principles that constrain the 'hypotheses' that learners can make and, in certain ways, their overall linguistic development.

Implicit

This complex and abstract system is also implicit as we know we have language in our heads, but we don't really know what the contents are. This implicit system is a vast network of forms and lexical items in our mind/ brain. A network is a map of grammatical and lexical items linked to each other through connections demonstrating relationships that are semantic (based on meaning such as the difference between *boring* and *interesting*), morphological (root word relationship such as *interest* and *interesting*) and formal (a relationship between one grammatical form that does not change the meaning of the root but when added produces a new word such as *boring* and *bored*). The network grows in our head as we process more language and make the right connections.

Sentences have an underlying hierarchical structure consisting of phrases (e.g. noun phrase (NP), verb phrase (VP), prepositional phrase (PP)) which require a 'head' and a 'complement'). To be clear, the 'head' is the element that determines the syntactic category of the phrase (for example, in a sentence like *Mahmoud teaches Math at the university*, 'Mahmoud' is the 'head' of the noun phrase, because this is the element that carries the 'nounness' in the noun phrase, whereas 'at' is the 'head' of the prepositional phrase 'at the university', because this is the element that carries the prepositional sense of the prepositional phrase) and the 'complement' is an optional element, or 'sister' (close to, in terms or relationship) to the 'head' (in the previous example, the whole prepositional phrase is the 'complement' of the verb phrase 'teaches' it accompanies or qualifies). This information is built into language learners' internal systems and learners make use of the input to process any possible variations in the target language. Instruction has no effect on this subconscious knowledge and second language learners create an abstract system (mental representation) similar to that of first language learners (the evidence overwhelmingly points toward the same mechanisms underlying language acquisition in both children and adults).

For example, sentences have an underlying hierarchical structure consisting of phrases, and these phrases require a head and a complement:

- Noun phrase (NP) = noun (head) + complement = Mahmoud *is professor*
- Verb phrase (VP) = verb (head) + complement = *teaches Math*
- Prepositional phrase (PP) = preposition (head) + complement = *at the American University of Sharjah*.

Learners do not need input to know that languages are hierarchical and consist of phrases. This comes automatically because such information is 'built' in (implicit) to the universal properties of languages. This representation bears little to no resemblance to what is traditionally taught and practised (grammatical rules). Language as mental representation builds up over time due to consistent and constant exposure to input data. It needs input to know whether there are variations between two languages. English is a head first language whereas Japanese is a head final language. Thus, for verb phrases, English follows verb (head) + complement (*Ahmad crashed the car*) while Japanese follows complement + verb (*Ahmad the car crashed*). This gives English the characteristic subject–verb–object word order while giving Japanese its characteristic subject object–verb word order. However, operations in both English and Japanese must observe the integrity of their phrases. Such variations are called parameters. Languages are shaped by parameters. In order for learners of English to build a system with head final if they learn Japanese, they need input to be able to interact mentally with universal properties and reset their parameters.

Language as mental representation refers to the complex abstract, constrained, implicit and underlying linguistic system in a speaker's mind/brain. It is implicit because we are not aware of it and we cannot describe its content with exact words. A rather different understanding and definition of language is the concept of language as a skill. The origins of this notion are grounded in the cognitive psychology perspective and refer to the speed and accuracy with which individuals perform certain actions. Skill is the ability to use language in real time (speaking, writing, listening and reading). It does involve the intersection of accuracy and fluency (speed in using the target language). Language learners acquire skills by participating in skill-based activities. Accuracy refers to how language learners can produce language error-free. Fluency instead refers to how (speed and confidence) L2 learners can perform an activity.

Despite the fact that language (mental representation) is internal in our minds/brains, when we speak or communicate we use it, and therefore we might think that language is also something external. However, communication and language are not the same thing. In short, communication is the external use of internal things, and one of those internal things is language.

The acquisition of grammatical properties is mainly implicit. Language is too abstract and complex to be taught and learnt explicitly. L2 learners create linguistic systems in an organised way that seem little affected by external forces such as instruction and correction. In short, language is not the rules and paradigms that appear on textbook pages. Explicit rules and paradigm lists can't become the abstract and complex system because the two things are completely different. What winds up in the human mind has no resemblance to anything on textbook pages or what teachers might say. This implication stems from the fact that there are no internal mechanisms that can convert explicit textbook rules into implicit mental representation.

Practice of the kind used in traditional grammar instruction does little to foster the development of mental representation and tends to develop a learning-like behaviour. Instruction does not have an effect on L2 learners implicit knowledge unless it is of a particular type that can facilitate acquisition. Instruction must therefore be devised in a way that, on one hand, enhances the grammatical features in the input, and on the other hand, provides L2 learners with opportunities to focus on meaning. L2 learners must be exposed to input and that input must be comprehensible and message-oriented in order to facilitate language development. Language that L2 learners hear and see in communicative contexts forms the data on which the internal mechanisms operate. The only effective way to facilitate language development (implicit knowledge) is the provision of good quality input.

So, how do we provide effective grammar instruction? L2 learners often expects to get presentation and explanation of grammar rules from language teachers. Language teachers often explain rules and this is followed by mechanical output practice (drills). However, let's quickly review basic facts about language and language development:

- Language is special and it is not learned in the same way as other complex mental phenomena. Humans are hardwired to learn language and have special cognitive mechanisms specifically designed to deal with language.
- Language is abstract and complex and should not be taught and learned explicitly. There is no mechanism that turns explicit rules into the abstract and complex mental representation we call 'language'.
- Language development is slow and piecemeal. L2 learners don't acquire one thing and then move on to another, as suggested by typical syllabi and textbooks. L2 learners' minds are constantly working on various aspects of language simultaneously. Only over time the internal system builds up and begins to resemble the second language.
- Language development is stage-like and ordered-like. In the acquisition of structure there are stages that all learners go through regardless of their L1. There is no evidence that stages can be skipped or orders can be altered.

- Language input provides the data for acquisition. Language that L2 learners hear and see in communicative contexts forms the data on which the internal mechanisms operate.

The question is therefore to determine what type of instruction is more successful in terms of helping L2 learners internalise the grammatical features of a target language. If we are going to instruct L2 learners on formal properties of the language in any way in the classroom, it ought to be input based and meaning oriented. This idea falls out of what we know about the nature of acquisition; that is, how it is tied to input within communicative settings and not explanation + practice.

The following principles should be considered in approaching grammar instruction:

(a) Instruction might help L2 learners to develop a good level of attainment particularly if opportunities to natural exposure to language input are given. Instruction has a facilitative role when it is used for linguistic features, which are not too distant from the learner's current level of language development (this is what Krashen called the 'i+1' level of input).

(b) Instruction might have a facilitative role in helping learners to pay selective attention to form and form-meaning connections in the input. Learners make form-meaning connections from the input they receive as they connect particular meanings to particular forms (grammatical or lexical). For example, they tend to connect a form with its meaning in the input they receive (the morpheme -*ato* on the end of a verb in Italian refers to an event in the past, as in 'parl-ato' *spoken*).

(c) Instruction should move from input to output practice. Initially, input-based and interactional options to instruction might help L2 learners to internalise the grammatical features of a target language. Structured input practice, for example, is a pedagogical intervention that through input manipulations facilitates the processing of grammatical and syntactic features of a target language. Textual enhancement is another pedagogical intervention through which the input is made more noticeable and eventually processable. Structured output tasks should follow input practice in grammar instruction.

Overall, the role of instruction in language acquisition is limited and constrained by a number of factors (e.g. orders and sequences of development, processing constraints). However, despite that instruction is, for instance, not able to alter the route of acquisition, it might have some beneficial effects in terms of speeding up the rate of language acquisition. The question is how. If we are going to focus on form in any way in the classroom, it ought to be input based and meaning oriented. Instruction as input manipulation might or might not facilitate language processing.

The empirical research measuring the effects of instruction is wobbly; that is, the results of the research are not always clear. One of the problems with the research is the way scholars measure outcomes of the pedagogical interventions. Just how do we know acquisition has happened after an intervention? Some scholars have argued that there is a huge bias toward explicit testing and tapping of explicit knowledge in the research on the role of instruction. What is more, given what we know about the slow and piecemeal nature of acquisition, it is hardly probable that instruction causes instantaneous acquisition of a particular property of language. In fact, it is probably *impossible*. That is, if we conduct one experiment, what do we really show in that one experiment? What is the nature of the treatment? How does the treatment reflect what we know about language development? What are we trying to alter in the learner? But researchers and teachers cling to the idea that we can make a difference in acquisition in some way by focusing on grammar. After all, isn't that what instruction is supposed to do? We propose that we are doing precisely that – making a difference – by providing a clear definition of language, by making a qualitative distinction between explicit and implicit knowledge (responsible for acquisition) and by attempting to measure implicit knowledge. Because of how language grows in the mind, the fact that language is implicit, complex and abstract, and communication develops over time, instruction must be designed to help the learner.

What are the main points?

Teachers keep teaching and worrying about rules that have no psychological validity. Language learners keep practising rules that have no psychological validity. Methods are twisted to fit the teaching of rules and patterns. Teachers have nothing to replace their notions of rules and patterns as they assume that any new approach for teaching language is simply a different way to teach the same thing.

Mental representation does not consist of rules. What every speaker/ knower of language creates in the mind/brain, is a complex, abstract and implicit representation of language. What we observe as 'language' is the result of a complex interaction of principles, constraints, and interfaces that yield utterances.

So what are the implications of this view about language for teachers and teaching?

- Language as mental representation is too abstract and complex to teach and learn explicitly. In short, language as mental representation is not the rules and paradigms that appear on textbook pages. Learners don't acquire rules but abstract properties. It is these abstract properties that cause verbs and adjectives for instance to do what they do in the language.
- Explicit rules and paradigm lists can't become the abstract and complex system because the two things are completely different. This implication stems from the fact that there is no internal mechanism that can convert explicit textbook rules into implicit mental representation. Comprehension-based approaches are the only ones that foster acquisition.
- There are aspects of language that cannot be learned (are innate or derived from universal properties). Learners do not acquire rules but process lexical and morphological forms and can internalise these units with their underlying features (e.g. the morphological manifestation of auxiliary *Does* in English).
- Teachers need to be armed with the knowledge that allows them to justify getting rid of traditional notions.

In traditional grammar-oriented instruction, one of the main assumptions is that language is learned through the deduction of the grammatical properties of second language and this allows learners to develop a conscious and explicit representation of that language in their internal grammatical system. Grammar instruction consists mainly of studying forms and structures with memorisation and translation of texts. It is also suggested that grammar is learned through the process of repetition, imitation and reinforcement. Grammatical structures are presented in a linear manner with no attention to meaning. These traditional approaches emphasise the use of memorisation and pattern drills as grammar teaching tasks and help to develop in the language learner a 'language-like behaviour'.

The so-called PPP (presentation–practice–production) proposes a three-stage model for language instruction. The first stage consists in the internalisation of a new form or structure which is usually presented through a text. The second stage implies the practice of the new form of structure through its systematic use. In the final stage activities are organised involving personal use of the target form or structure. The PPP suggests the use of activities which allow the learner to move from systematic to appropriate use of the language in contexts. It is only when learners have mastered the form that they will be able to use it in context where the message becomes more important than the medium. A traditional grammar-oriented approach is often characterised by paradigmatic explanations of specific linguistic forms or structures. The paradigmatic explanation is followed by pattern practice and substitution drills. In this type of mechanical practice (see examples below), real life situations are completely ignored and practice is implemented in a completely decontextualised way.

> 'Today we are going to learn about past tense forms. Does anyone know what the past tense is, how it is formed and how we use it? (silence from the class) Well, the past tense in Italian is formed by … (present the class with a paradigm of past tense). For example in this sentence we add/change … (quizzical look from students)…What is the past tense of the verb "to go"? If I need to say "Yesterday I went to the cinema with a friend" how do you say this in Italian? (one student ventures an answer) … '

Mechanical drills are problematic for three main reasons:

(i)   They force language learners to produce grammatical forms before they are capable of comprehending the forms, which leads to incorrect generalisations and overuse of the form when not necessary. Learners need the opportunity to comprehend language before being able to use it accurately.

(ii)   They don't allow learners to make form-meaning connections in comprehension and production. The idea that acquiring grammar can be achieved simply by learning about the grammatical rules of a target language and practising those rules through production tasks (very often mechanical and traditional) has been challenged by many scholars in the field of second language acquisition.

(iii) They don't allow learners those aspects (surface features) of language that are individual to languages and can be learnt by exposure (lexical and morphological forms).

Keeping in mind the nature of language, rather than teaching about the language, we should look at how we can create the necessary conditions to facilitate language acquisition. Input manipulation facilitates and fosters language acquisition (lexical and morphological forms). Unlike traditional instruction, where the focus of instruction is in the explanation of rules and manipulation of learners' output simply facilitating the development of a 'language-like behaviour', comprehension-based pedagogical interventions, such as processing instruction, are aimed at changing the way input is perceived and processed by language learners facilitating the acquisition of lexical and morphological surface features.

Processing instruction, the cognitive process which occurs when input is understood and integrated into the language, is predicated on the input processing theory. Input processing refers to the fact that language learners are exposed to input which contains linguistic forms. Processing instruction is not about rule learning but it is about processing behaviour and its relationship with the acquisition of surface features. When language learners process input, they have limited resources to ensure that they make correct form-meaning connections (when they hear a sentence such as *I talked to my teacher*, and understand that *talked* means that the action is in the past, a form-meaning connection is made). Learners cannot just notice the form, as they need to comprehend the meaning that the particular form encodes. Learners make use of two main processing strategies when they are exposed to language input:

(i)   they first process input for meaning before they process the linguistic form. The result of this will be that learners will not make natural connections between forms in the input and their meanings;

(ii) they will tend to process the first noun or pronoun they encounter in a sentence as the subject or agent. The result of this will be that learners will misinterpret sentences in which the first element in a sentence is not the subject or agent.

Processing instruction aims at altering the processing strategies/principles learners take to the task of comprehension and to encourage them to make better form-meaning connections than they would if left to their own devices. Through structured input activities, language learners are pushed to process the form or structure. In structured input activities the input is manipulated in particular ways to make learners become dependent on form and structure to get meaning. Processing instruction is focused on the development of mental representation of language. It is not a pedagogical intervention meant to assist in skill development. It is not concerned with the teaching of rules but with the processing of morpho-phonological units in input strings.

There is a view among teachers and practitioners that language is represented by the rules and explanations found in language textbooks. Some of the myths perpetuated by this view include that explicitly teaching grammar is necessary and that practice makes perfect. When we discussed the nature of language, it was argued that providing explicit information and giving rules does not facilitates the acquisition of language. A working definition of language is that it is a complex, abstract, constrained and implicit system that exists in a speaker's head. Explicit and metalinguistic knowledge are not part of language as mental representation.

Language acquisition is not driven by explicit rules but by interaction with input data and universal principles. Input must be comprehensible, message oriented and easy to process to have an effect on our internal acquisition mechanisms and to facilitate the acquisition of surface features. Language development is affected by linguistics and processing constraints.

In traditional instruction, language learners are provided with long and elaborate grammatical explanations of target language grammatical rules (paradigms). This explicit information is normally followed by mechanical output drill practice. A more effective way to incorporate instruction and facilitate language development is through input-manipulation pedagogical interventions such as processing instruction.

In this pocket guide, we argue that the product of acquisition is an abstract, complex, constrained and implicit system called 'language' that defies easy explanation and looks nothing like textbook rules or descriptions language learners might find in a Google search.

What else can we read?

Benati (2020) *Key Questions in Language Teaching.* Cambridge: Cambridge University Press.

Benati, A. (2017) Classroom-oriented research: Processing Instruction (findings and implications). *Language Teaching,* 52: 343–59. https://doi.org/10.1017/s0261444817000386

Benati, A. (2014) Second Language Acquisition. In Fäcke, C. (ed), *Language Acquisition* (179–97). New York: Mouton de Gruyter.

Benati, A. (2013) *Key Issues in Second Language Teaching.* London: Equinox.

Benati, A. and Schwieter, J. (2019) Pedagogical interventions to L2 grammar instruction. In Schwieter, J. and Benati, A. (eds), *The Cambridge Handbook of Language Learning* (475–99). Cambridge: Cambridge University Press.

VanPatten, B. (2015) Foundations of processing. *International Review of Applied Linguistics,* 53: 91–109. https://doi.org/10.1515/iral-2015-0005

VanPatten, B., Smith, M. and Benati, A. (2019) *Key Questions in Second Language Acquisition: An Introduction.* Cambridge: Cambridge University Press.

VanPatten, B. and Benati, A. (2015) *Second Language Acquisition: Key Terms* (2nd edn). London: Bloomsbury.

VanPatten, B. and Rothman, J. (2014) Against rules. In Benati, A., Laval, C. and Arche, M. (eds), *The Grammar Dimension in Instructed Second Language Learning* (15–35). London: Bloomsbury.

Wong, W. (2005) *Input Enhancement: From Theory and Research to the Classroom.* New York: McGraw-Hill.

10 Language Tasks

Can we take a minute to think about this?

One of the key questions in language teaching is: can language practice be equated to a language task? Practice *must be* distinguished from a language task. A misleading assumption in language teaching is that drill mechanical practice is effective. Explicit information about language rules and rules practice through exercises *do not have* a positive effect on language as mental representation. Language teachers often work in the dark, with little understanding of the object of their efforts and often lacking a clear understanding of the role and nature of language. Curriculum and language teaching materials must be genuinely informed by what we know about language and language acquisition and embrace a language task approach.

Tasks are the quintessential communicative event in contemporary language teaching. They are both meaningful and have a communicative purpose. The exact definition of a task varies somewhat among scholars but at the kernel of all definitions you'll find the following:

- A language task is not mere language practice.
- A language task involves the expression, interpretation and negotiation of meaning.

However, the lack of knowledge about what a task is and how it can be implemented effectively, leads to misleading claims and misunderstanding:

- Speaking in another language is not just about developing the ability to use grammar correctly, to access vocabulary and pronounce words correctly (linguistic competence). It is also the ability to understand when, why and in what ways to produce language (communicative competence).
- Traditional approaches to listening comprehension encourage passive listening. In the traditional practice of listening comprehension, L2 learners listen to the teacher or to a recorded audio

clip and they are usually asked to answer questions related to the text or to fill in the gap activity. The gap usually highlights the linguistic elements rather than the communicative elements in the passage.

- Traditional approaches to reading comprehension reduce reading to a mere exercise of 'reading and translating' and/or 'reading and answering questions'.
- Traditional approaches to writing have focused on the texts that writers produce. In doing so, writing is simply reduced to a matter of translating preconceived ideas into a text.

What is the nature and role of language tasks?

A task is a language-learning endeavour that requires the L2 learner to (a) comprehend, (b) manipulate, and (c) produce the target language as they perform some set of work plans. Tasks provide learners with a purpose for language use and make language teaching more communicative. Tasks are activities which involve understanding and processing of the target language.

Language tasks have specific features:

- They provide a piece of extended discourse.
- They have an information gap element.
- They have an uncertainty element.
- They are goal orientated.
- They are real-time processing.
- They require two or more autonomous participants.
- They privilege L2 learners' use of the language.

In order to create a communicative and effective the following criteria should be adopted:

- Identify a desired informational outcome.
- Break down the topic into subtopics.
- Create and sequence concrete tasks (steps) for L2 learners to do, for example create lists, fill in charts, make tables.

- Build in linguistic support, either lexical or grammatical or both (the teacher is the resource person and the architect who is planning the task and learners are the executor).

If a language task follows the above criteria and it is structured in an appropriate way it can successfully promote communication among L2 learners. Tasks promote communication but the question is to whether they also have a beneficial role for second language acquisition. It can be argued that it can facilitate language acquisition processes in a number of ways.

First, in interactive tasks, L2 learners receive and are exposed to meaningful input from a variety of sources: teachers; other learners; and the task itself. More importantly, the input – both aural and written – is made comprehensible and meaningful. The input language learners are exposed to is simplified (e.g. short utterances, forms are made salient, the language is simplified). These modifications help language learners to process the language, and it increases the chances of improvement in their internal language developing system.

Second, in interactive tasks, L2 learners are not engaged in mechanical output practice (e.g. drills, repetition exercises) where the language they produce is not meaningful. Interactive tasks instead allow language learners to engage in meaningful production of language which can help them in filling the gaps in their knowledge (forms, words and structures to convey meaning) and facilitating language acquisition.

Third, in interactive tasks, the focus is not just on expression and interpretation of meaning but also on negotiation of meaning. Providing language learners with opportunities to negotiate meaning (e.g. confirmation checks) increases the amount of language input that is comprehended and therefore facilitates learning.

Speaking is an interactive process of constructing meaning that involves producing, receiving and processing information. All communicative tasks must ensure L2 learners develop their ability to share information, negotiate meaning and interact with others. Speaking tasks must be developed with the intention of promoting communication and communicative language use.

A language task is a learning endeavour that requires L2 learners to comprehend, negotiate, manipulate and produce the target language as they need to perform a set of work plans. L2 learners must develop their ability to manage interaction as well as engage in the negotiation of meaning. The management of the interaction involves such things as when and how to take the floor, when to introduce a topic or change the subject, how to invite someone else to speak, how to keep a conversation going and so on. Negotiation of meaning refers to the skill of making sure the person you are speaking to has correctly understood you and that you have correctly understood them.

Speaking interactive tasks

How do we develop effective oral interactive tasks? A series of measures needs to be considered in order to achieve this.

First, language instructors should develop group oral tasks which increase language learners' talk time and at the same time lower the inhibitions of L2 learners who are unwilling to speak in front of the full class. In group work, learners perform a learning task through small-group interaction. One of the advantages of group interaction is that it can foster learner responsibility and independence, and it can improve motivation and contribute to effective and careful organisation/planning.

Second, language instructors should base the oral task on easy and comprehensible language that will help learners to produce target language with the minimum of hesitation.

Third, language instructors should keep L2 learners speaking the target language and they should monitor the learners' use of the target language at all times during their tasks. L2 learners should be allowed to initiate communication, and speaking tasks should involve negotiation for meaning. Positive corrective feedback on learners' performance should be carefully provided.

Fourth, language instructors should choose an interesting and familiar topic which enables learners to use and tap into their ideas from their own experience and knowledge.

Fifth, language instructors should provide clear instruction to accomplish the task. In group or pair-work everyone in the group contributes to the discussion. L2 learners must take initiative and responsibility to complete the task. L2 learners need to take the initiative and make decisions in order to complete the task successfully.

Sixth, language instructors should create a classroom environment where L2 learners have real-life authentic communication, and meaningful tasks that promote speaking skills. This can occur when students collaborate in groups to achieve a goal or to complete a task. L2 learners must be given a task where they need something to talk about and someone to talk to.

Seventh, teachers should develop a task that is essentially goal-oriented and that requires the group or pair to achieve an objective that is usually expressed by an observable result, such as brief notes or lists, a rearrangement of jumbled items, a drawing, or a spoken summary. In designing a task, we must make sure that learners collect data through interaction and production speech tasks designed for a specific purpose. These are the five key components of language tasks:

1   Goal: the general purpose of the task.
2   Input: the verbal or non-verbal information supplied with the task (e.g. pictures; a map; written text).
3   Conditions: the way in which the information is presented (e.g. split vs. shared information), or the way in which it is to be used (e.g. converging vs. diverging).
4   Procedures: the methodological procedures to be followed in performing the task (e.g. group vs. pair work).
5   Predicted outcomes: the 'product' that results from completing the task (e.g. a route drawn in on a map; a list of differences between two pictures).

In structuring the so-called information exchange tasks, language instructors should adopt the following criteria:

- They should identify a desired information outcome.
- They should identify information sources.
- They should create and sequence concrete tasks for learners to complete.
- They should build in linguistic support.

Information exchange tasks should substitute traditional oral practice task where L2 learners are asked to talk about a specific topic 'How do you spend your free time and over the weekend?' In these kinds of activity (open ended question activity type) learners will have very little to talk about and few opportunities to interact.

Identify a desired information outcome. This is the first element to consider in developing an effective exchange information task. The main informational goal of the task needs to be determined. In other words, we need to establish what specific questions L2 learners will be able to answer at the end of the task.

Identify information sources. Information that L2 learners need to exchange comes from two main sources: from themselves (e.g. their views, their opinions, etc.); and from outside sources (e.g. texts, programs, etc.).

Create and sequence concrete tasks for L2 learners to complete. Once goals are established, the interactive task is made of different steps/stages. Steps/stages are set so that L2 learners can meet the goals of the task.

Build in linguistic support. L2 learners need to be provided with the appropriate linguistic support to complete the task. The question language instructors need to ask is: Would they have the sufficient vocabulary to complete the various steps of the task?

Listening comprehension interactive tasks

In the case of the type of classroom tasks which might facilitate the development of listening comprehension skills, classroom research suggests that listening tasks should be well-structured to allow active participation and interaction from the listener. Task types can be classified in different ways and in the next section we will examine some of these listening comprehension tasks. In an interactive approach to listening comprehension, L2 learners play the role of active listeners. They listen to a passage to understand and they are required to understand the meaning conveyed. In this more communicative approach to listening comprehension tasks, language teachers should help L2 learners to develop a series of listening strategies (e.g. listening for the gist, listening for purpose, etc., see a list and examples of key strategies below) and the ability to use them in different listening situations.

In adopting a principled and evidence-based approach to the teaching of listening comprehension, a series of factors need to be taken into consideration in order to foster the development of listening skills:

Key strategies

Listening for the gist: Is the passage about describing living in the city or living in the countryside? Is it a positive or negative view about the current political situation?

Listening for purpose: Is the speaker buying a ticket or making an enquiry? Does John agree or disagree with the death penalty?

Listening for main concepts: Does the speaker like or dislike President Obama? Did John like or dislike the book?

Listening for specific: How much did the room cost? What time does John meet with Laura?

(a) The role of L2 learners
(b) L2 learners' strategies
(c) The type of listening tasks used

L2 learners are generally engaged in listening tasks that are either collaborative or non-collaborative (particularly in the language laboratory). The main challenge is to develop listening tasks which will stimulate the development of listening skills while ensuring L2 learners make use of their own listening strategies (e.g. to listen for specific information, obtain information for a specific purpose, inferencing and personalising). Language teachers also need to ensure that L2 learners are engaged in listening tasks where they make use of bottom-up and top-down strategies. Below is a list of normal tendencies that successful language listeners might display when processing language:

- They tend to predict what they might hear or what might happen.
- They tend to guess what they might have heard or what the speakers might have said.
- They tend to focus on key words and select key information.
- They tend to monitor their understanding of the meaning of what they hear.
- They tend to reflect on what they heard and attempt to formulate an opinion, and/or to interact with a speaker, or to personalise the content.

The basic constructive strategies that successful L2 listeners tend to adopt when they encounter some uncertainty are:

- Predicting: using real-world expectations to generate predictions about what the speakers will say and what might happen.
- Guessing: making inferences about what the speakers might have said or might have meant, even when 'bottom up' information about the language may be incomplete.
- Selecting: focusing on key words, trying to select targeted information that is adequate to complete a given task.
- Clarifying: monitoring one's level of understanding and identifying questions that can be asked to supplement partial understanding or correct misunderstanding, and revising one's representation of meaning.
- Responding: reacting or attempting to formulate an opinion, to interact with the speaker, to personalise the content, focus on what was understood, attempt to talk about the input or conversation in a comfortable way.

If we teach these strategies explicitly and persistently, and if we incorporate their use directly into our listening tasks, we will help L2 learners gain control over the listening process. When we develop a listening task, we should consider all these strategies and incorporate their use directly into our listening tasks.

Now if we look at listening in the language classroom the two main questions to be asked are:

1   What kind of listening tasks should L2 learners be engaged with in the classroom?
2   Do they have the opportunity to use and develop their skills and strategies during the listening tasks?

In order to answer the above questions appropriately and to ensure that language instructors develop listening tasks which integrate listening skills, we need to consider the following steps:

(a) Language teachers should develop listening tasks that have a specific communicative purpose.

(b) Language teachers should choose topics that are familiar and interesting for language learners. They must be able to extract meaning from the text. In order to do that, they need to figure out the main purpose of their listening.

(c) Language teachers need to design a listening task which will activate learners' background knowledge about the specific topic so that they will be able to predict the content of the task and to use appropriate listening strategies in order to complete it.

(d) Language teachers need to contextualise the listening task. They need to provide clues to meaning. They need to provide the listener with an idea of the type of information to expect and what to do with before the actual listening begins.

(e) Language teachers need to define the task's instructional goal and type of response expected. Each listening and comprehension task should have as its goal the improvement of one or more specific listening skills.

(f) Language teachers should spell out the goal(s) of a listening comprehension task (e.g. recognising specific aspects of the message, such as sounds, words, morphological distinctions; determining the topic about a message; comprehending main ideas).

(g) Language teachers should take into consideration the level of difficulty of the listening comprehension passage by considering the following factors: how the information is presented; how familiar learners are with the topic; whether the listening task offers visual support (e.g. maps, diagrams, pictures).

(h) Language teachers should make use of pre-listening tasks to prepare students for what they are going to hear or view. Pre-listening tasks activate learners' knowledge and interest. The pre-listening tasks assess learners' background knowledge, and provide them with the background knowledge necessary for coping with language comprehension (e.g. reviewing relevant vocabulary or grammatical structures before listening to a passage; reading something relevant to the listening task; predicting the content of the listening text, think-pair share, brainstorming). Pre-listening tasks help students make decisions about what to listen for and, subsequently, to focus their attention on meaning while listening. Language teachers need to raise learners' consciousness/knowledge of the relevant topic. They also need to establish a listening purpose so that learners know the specific information they need to listen for, and they can make predictions to anticipate what they might hear.

(i) Language teachers should encourage the development of L2 learners' listening strategies by exposing learners to different ways of processing information such as bottom-up tasks (e.g. word sentence recognition, listening for different morphological endings), top-down tasks (identifying the topic, understanding the meaning of the sentence), and interactive tasks (e.g. listening to a list and categorising the words, following directions).

(j) Language teachers must expose L2 learners to a variety of tasks in order to develop listening strategies such as looking for key words, looking for non-verbal cues to meaning, associating information with one existing background knowledge (activating schemata), guessing meanings, listening for the general gist, seeking clarification. Tasks, where learners need to extrapolate meaning, can be grouped according to the response learners must produce. The two main categories are: Listening tasks where learners perform physical tasks; Listening tasks where learners transfer information.

The notion of task is central to language learning and teaching. In listening tasks, the 'post-listening' stage of listening occurs in the few minutes following the actual exposure to the text. Effective listening tasks often involve an explicit 'pre-listening' step, which consists of some activities that the learner does prior to listening to the main input in order to increase readiness. This step is designed to activate what the learner already knows, provide an 'advance organiser' to help L2 learners predict ideas and 'pre-structure' information.

An interactive listening comprehension task should have the following characteristics:

- In the pre-listening phase, language teachers should set the context, create motivation and activate L2 learners' prior knowledge through cooperative learning task (e.g. brainstorming, think–pair–share). Effective listening tasks involve learners in predicting ideas and pre-structuring relevant information in the text. Pre-listening tasks include vocabulary learning and/or identifying key ideas contained in the upcoming input.

- In the while-listening phase, L2 learners are required to listen for main ideas to establish the context and transferring information. Learners are exposed to listening bottom-up tasks (e.g. word sentence recognition, listening for different morphological ending), top-down tasks (identifying the topic, understanding the meaning of a sentence) and interactive tasks (e.g. listening to a list and categorising the words, following directions). Main listening tasks at this stage include guided note-taking, and completion of a picture, or schematic diagram or table.

- The post-listening phase helps learners to examine the functional language and infer the meaning of vocabulary (e.g. guess the meaning of unknown vocabulary, analyse the success of communication in the script, brainstorm alternative ways of expression). In the final stage, language learners are given post-listening tasks which involve reading, writing, speaking, and interaction activities.

The nature and role of reading comprehension

Reading is considered an interactive process between the reader and the text and results in comprehension. The text presents letters, words, sentences, and paragraphs that encode meaning. The reader uses knowledge, skills, and strategies to determine what that meaning is. Readers need to develop the ability to recognise the elements of the writing system (e.g. word recognition, grammatical features); they need to develop knowledge of discourse and how different parts of the text connect with each other; they need to develop a knowledge of different types of texts; and the need to be able to use top-down and bottom-up strategies. Developing reading comprehension skills can be defined as the reader's ability to use and apply appropriate skills and strategies in order to successfully comprehend a written text.

Research on word recognition has indicated that recognising a word is a necessary component in comprehending a text. However, it is not sufficient to develop full comprehension. Readers must construct meaning from the words he/she can recognise. Language teachers should provide guided practice in reading in order to increase learner's comprehension.

Good readers must develop good vocabulary knowledge. Language teachers must provide multiple exposures to vocabulary.

Developing learners' comprehension is the process of constructing meaning from a text. It involves word knowledge (vocabulary) as well as thinking and reasoning. This process involves making use of learners' prior knowledge. It involves drawing from internal strategies to process words and expressions in the input learners hear. Likewise, in the development of listening skills, reading skills are affected by two processing strategies: bottom-up, and top-down. Bottom-up strategies are used by learners to gradually decode the linguistics information (e.g. orthographic knowledge, lexical and syntactic knowledge) in a written text – from the small to large units. Readers process letters and characters, and analyse and interpret the meaning of words and sentences. Top-down strategies involve processing beyond the analysis of linguistics information (e.g. knowledge of text structure), and prior knowledge (e.g. topics familiarity, culture awareness). The so-called Schema Theory suggests that, as learners, our knowledge impacts on how we process and understand new incoming information. Research in reading has provided the following insights for developing reading skills:

- L2 learners benefit from pre-reading activities that are very effective in improving schema activation and use of reading strategies.
- L2 learners should be exposed to reading for a real-life specific purpose.
- L2 learners should read extensively.
- L2 learners should be encouraged to integrate information in the text with existing knowledge.
- L2 learners should be motivated and should engage in reading tasks with a specific purpose.
- L2 learners should be engaged in tasks stimulating different skills (e.g. perceptual processing, phonemic processing).

L2 learners tend not to transfer the strategies they use when reading in their native language to reading in another language. When reading a text from another language they exclusively rely on their linguistic knowledge (a bottom-up strategy). One of the language instructors' challenges is to help learners not to rely on this bottom-up strategy and use top-down strategies as they do in their native language. Some of these strategies can help learners to read effectively in the language they are learning. Previewing of a text might help learners to develop a general understanding of the content of a passage.

Using readers' pre existing knowledge might help in making predictions about content, discourse structure, vocabulary and main concepts in a text. Skimming and scanning might help learners to get the main ideas in the text and confirm or question predictions.

Guessing from context might help learners to decode the meanings of unknown words rather than translating word by word. Paraphrasing might help learners to summarise the main ideas and concepts in a text using their own words.

Language instructors can help learners to use these reading strategies in several ways. They can take L2 learners through the processes of previewing, predicting, skimming and scanning, and paraphrasing. They should allow enough time in classroom for group previewing and predicting activities in preparation for a reading comprehension task. They should develop tasks that encourage learners to guess meaning from context. When language learners are able to use reading strategies, they will be able to effectively develop their ability to read in another language. There are issues related to topic interest, language difficulty and topic familiarity, addressed by scholars in second language acquisition which account for a significant variation in comprehension. Learners find it difficult to process complex language and unfamiliar topics. Therefore, it is desirable for teachers to select a text according to learners' topic familiarity.

An effective way to improve L2 learners' reading comprehension abilities is for language instructors to help them develop reading strategies that they can use in different reading tasks. Reading is a key part of language instruction as it supports learning in multiple ways. When learners are exposed to a variety of materials to read, they have many opportunities to process vocabulary, grammar, and sentence structure in authentic contexts. Also, L2 learners develop a better picture of how these elements of the language work together to convey meaning. Reading for content information in the language classroom provides learners with both authentic reading material and an authentic purpose for reading. When reading to learn, students need to follow four basic steps:

1   Figure out the purpose for reading. Activate background knowledge of the topic in order to predict or anticipate content and identify appropriate reading strategies.
2   Attend to the parts of the text that are relevant to the identified purpose and ignore the rest. This selectivity enables students to focus on specific items in the input and reduces the amount of information they have to process and hold in short-term memory.
3   Select strategies that are appropriate to the reading task and use them flexibly and interactively. Students' comprehension improves and their confidence increases when they use top-down and bottom-up skills simultaneously to construct meaning.
4   Check comprehension while reading and when the reading task is completed. Monitoring comprehension helps students detect inconsistencies and comprehension failures, helping them learn to use alternate strategies.

Reading comprehension interactive tasks

The pedagogical implication of the Schema Theory is the understanding that reading is an interactive process between readers and texts. Readers must associate elements in a text with their pre-reading knowledge. Reading activities in traditional textbooks consist mainly of two types:

- Translation tasks (read a passage and translate into French)
- Answer questions from a text (a typical task/exercise is: Read the dialogue/text and answer the following questions).

Reading should be viewed as reading in another language rather than as an exercise in translation. The fact that language learners do not necessarily have the verbal virtuosity of a native reader means language teachers need to use some strategies to help them. The framework presented here takes into consideration the need to guide learners in their comprehension of a text. In adopting a principled evidence-based approach to the teaching of reading skills, a series of measures need to be taken into consideration. Language teachers should develop reading activities following a five-stage approach:

- Pre-reading stage
- Reading stage

- Text-interaction stage
- Post-reading stage
- Personalisation stage.

When designing a reading task, language instructors must keep in mind that we cannot expect learners to process all the information in a text. The purpose of the reading comprehension tasks is to bridge the gap between the reader and the information contained in the text. The tasks follow a five-stage approach with a pre-reading stage, a reading stage, a text-interaction stage, a post-reading stage and a personalisation stage.

Developing reading comprehension skills involves the interaction of a variety of knowledge sources. An interactive model for the comprehension of written language has been proposed. This model envisages that L2 learners make a positive contribution to their learning. The proposed framework for developing reading comprehension tasks comprises of different stages. Based on the principles highlighted in this chapter, instructors should be supplied with the following guidelines for the development of effective reading comprehension tasks:

- Reading comprehension tasks should be constructed around a purpose that has significance for learners. This will stimulate their motivation and interest.
- Reading comprehension tasks should be developed by language instructors for a specific purpose and language instructors should make sure that L2 learners understand what the purpose of reading is. A task can have more than one instructional purpose (e.g. practising a specific grammatical structure, introducing new vocabulary, familiarising learners with a particular topic); Reading comprehension tasks should have a defined goal and develop tasks for learners to deliver appropriate responses.
- Use pre-reading tasks activities to prepare students for reading and to activate their background knowledge.
- Use text-interaction reading tasks to gradually bridge the gap between the text and the reader.
- Use post-reading tasks to check and verify comprehension.
- Use personalisation tasks to encourage learners to exploit the communicative function of the reading text.

Developing effective writing tasks

One of the major developments in second language pedagogy has been the shift from product-oriented approaches to process-oriented approaches in the teaching of language writing skills. Process-oriented approaches focus on the creation of a text rather than concentrating only on the final product. Writing, like any other aspects of second language development, is about communication. In real life we write e-mails, notes, letters, grocery lists, reports, essays. All these different tasks have a communicative purpose and a specific audience.

A communicative task-based approach to the development of writing skills is proposed in this chapter as an effective option in teaching writing. This approach takes into consideration a cognitive-process theory of writing. Writing is a somewhat neglected skill in second language teaching and, very often, writing tasks set up by language teachers might not be motivating for language learners and not properly incorporated into a language lesson. In order to develop more effective tasks for developing writing skills, language teachers must clarify the communicative purpose of the written task and the target audience. Language teachers must consider the use of more meaningful, realistic and relevant writing tasks based on what L2 learners need.

The development of writing skills will help L2 learners to gain independence, fluency and creativity in language writing. In developing writing skills, L2 learners improve the way they put their thoughts into words in a meaningful and accurate way to convey a specific message. Writing is a process where language learners explore, consolidate and develop specific objectives. The same definition used for communication is applicable to the written language. Through writing learners are able to communicate information to a wider audience.

What is the main role of writing in language teaching? First of all, writing has a role in helping learners to acquire the target language. Teachers might design writing activities to make L2 learners learn new vocabulary for example. Secondly, writing can be used to produce a text in a real-life context (e.g. writing an e-mail, producing a poster … etc.).

Traditional writing practice is often reduced to practice structures or vocabulary that has just been learned. The role of writing should involve creating content and tailoring this content in relation to writers' needs. Writing involves a complex interaction between a wide range of different processes and L2 learners adopt specific strategies to cope with the task of writing. Before starting to write, L2 learners must define the rhetorical problem:

- The reason/s for writing
- The purpose of the text to be written
- The recipient of the written text
- The topic
- The learners' knowledge about the topic.

Furthermore, L2 learners should plan the writing very carefully. Planning writing should involve a number of sub-processes such as: planning the composition, generating ideas, organising ideas and setting goals. This brief description of the processes involved in writing tells us how dynamic and complex writing is, regardless of whether the learner writes in his/her mother tongue or other languages.

A cognitive and processing second language instruction model emphasises L2 learner mental processes in writing. Cognitive processes in writing engage L2 learners in exploring, consolidating and developing rhetorical objectives. The act of writing involves three major elements:

1   The task environment which includes things outside the writer knowledge such as the rhetorical problem and the text itself.
2   The writer's long-term memory which includes the knowledge that learners might have about the topic, the audience for which the text is going to be written, and its various writing plans.
3   The writing processes which involve three basic processes: planning; translating plans into a text; and reviewing, which includes reading and editing the text produced.

The planning process contains four sub-processes:

(a)   Generating ideas, which includes retrieving information from long-term memory
(b)   Searching for ideas
(c)   Reaching a specific audience
(d)   Setting a goal for the writing.

The translating process includes the ability to put ideas into words. It requires the writer to juggle all the various demands of the new language.

The reviewing process depends on two sub-processes:

- Evaluating
- Revising.

In traditional instruction, writing practice has focused on the texts that writers produce. In doing so, writing is simply reduced to a matter of translating preconceived ideas into a text. In current language textbooks written activities often focus on production of grammatical and lexical structures. Learners are provided with a list of words which they must use to write a short paragraph or a series of sentences. It can be argued that in this task the rhetorical problem for learners is simply reduced to producing a text using grammatical and lexical items.

The focus of this exercise is only to produce a text that contains particular lexical and grammatical items. The processes involved in traditional writing activities are minimal as the content is not as important as the accurate use of specific linguistic items. Planning consists of constructing and ordering individual sentences. Reviewing focuses on which linguistic items have been used.

Traditional approaches to the teaching of L2 writing have mainly focused on linguistic rules and vocabulary.

Process-oriented approaches have shifted the focus onto the audience and the purpose of writing. Using communicative composing-oriented written tasks that engage learners in authentic and interactive writing activities is what language teachers should consider. These types of tasks aim to improve learners' writing skills and consist of three main phases:

- Pre-writing phase
- Writing phase
- Focus on language phase.

In developing and designing writing tasks language teachers should consider the following questions:

- What is the purpose of the written task?
- Does the task engage learners positively?

- Is the task interesting and familiar?
- Does it focus on a specific genre?
- Does it integrate other skills such as reading and speaking?
- Is there enough support provided to students to be successful in the task?

Writing interactive tasks

In developing writing tasks, teachers should consider the following:

- Writing tasks need to reflect authentic purposes.
- Writing tasks should have clear guidance and a scaffolding approach.

There are different types of tasks that can be used to enhance students' writing skills:

- Matching: listening and writing, matching phrases/description to pictures, matching directions to maps.
- Comparing: finding similarities or differences.
- Problem-solving: real-life situations, case studies, incomplete texts.
- Projects and creative tasks: doing and reporting a survey, producing a class newspaper, planning a radio show, designing a brochure.
- Sharing personal experiences: story-telling, anecdotes, memories, opinions, reactions.
- Ordering and sorting: sequencing, ranking, classifying.
- Listing: brainstorming and/or fact finding.

A three-stage approach in designing a written task should therefore be adopted to teach how to write in a second language: Pre-writing; Writing; Language Focus. This approach would improve L2 learners' writing skills as they will become better at formulating their ideas in a coherent way, using correct syntax, grammar and vocabulary.

- Pre-writing phase in which L2 learners are given different options so that they can make choices and decide in which direction to develop their composition.
- Writing stage that begins immediately after the previous phase and during which L2 learners become aware of the elements of good writing.
- Language focus.

The pre-writing-phase

In the pre-writing phase the topic and the specific task are introduced. L2 learners have a chance to recall things that they know. The teacher might decide to show a picture, audio or video in relation to the topic. The teacher can also elicit appropriate vocabulary or phrases which students might find useful. During this time, L2 learners are expected to work in pairs to decide the nature of their writing task and the composition. Then, they begin drafting. During this period, the teacher should urge them to let their ideas flow onto the paper without concern for accuracy in producing the target language (e.g. forms, structures).

The writing-phase

The language teacher should be merely a facilitator in the writing process and ensure learners are supported in their effort to become good writers in a second language. Once the teacher knows that L2 learners have developed an interest in writing, they can provide them with meaningful opportunities to write for different audiences and for different purposes using a variety of genres (e.g. stories, biographical pieces, essays). The writing phase is divided into three stages: (a) the task itself; (b) the planning stage; (c) and the report stage.

(a) The task phase should not be repetitive and must have a communicative goal for the writer to achieve. For example, making an important decision about buying a car, writing a list of items that may be needed to organise a picnic, or writing a plan for a party. The main purpose of the task is to allow writers to use their own ideas without worrying about grammar, spelling and other mechanics in a target language. There should be no restriction on the language to be used. The focus is on communicating meaning rather than using forms at this stage.

(b)   The planning stage involves language writers working with the teacher to improve their writing skills. Here, there is a heavy emphasis on form-focused instruction as learners attempt to improve the overall correctness of their writing.

(c)   At the report stage, language writers present their findings and the teacher's role is to act as a chairperson to summarise each writer's work and make comments about the written text.

Language Focus

This is the final stage of the writing task and it allows a closer look at some of the specific features occurring in the language used during the writing phase. By this time, learners will have already worked with the language and processed it for meaning, so that they are ready to concentrate more closely on formal properties of the language. An example for a writing task is to ask L2 learners to re-write a story recalling the story from a listening passage. This task helps students clarify their understanding of the story and gives them more practice in using the language. See below some guidelines used to prepare such a task:

- The teacher should consider a short story that is easy to understand. The teachers need to ensure that learners understand the meaning of the key words.
- The teacher should select key words from the story that the writer can use later (cues) to reconstruct the story.
- The teacher may first listen to the story and ask learners to focus on the main ideas and the key words.
- The teacher should ask learners to take turns (after they listen to the story) with another learner in the class to tell each other the story using their own words.
- The teachers should encourage learners to make use of the key words.
- The teachers should ask learners to write down what they remember from the listening, using key words from the story.
- The teacher may collect the written work of learners for comments and improvement.

Developing writing is a key component in developing learners' ability to communicate in a second language. A composing-oriented approach challenges the way written tasks are practised in a traditional approach. Likewise, in the listening and reading tasks proposed in previous chapters, a similar step-by step approach is proposed for developing learners' writing skills.

What are the main points?

To recap, the main points are:

- Design clear tasks that focus on meaning. A task is designed for the purposes of increasing learning, exposing learners to meaningful input. A task should have a clear set of procedures, and it can be monitored and evaluated by the language instructor.
- Maximise acquisition by creating pre-listening tasks (e.g. pre-listening surveys, pair questionnaires, or prediction activities using key vocabulary from the extract) that activate learners' knowledge and interest.
- While-listening tasks can include guided note-taking, completion of a picture or schematic diagram or table, composing questions and any tangible activity that the learner does while listening to demonstrate ongoing monitoring of meaning.
- The post-listening phase occurs in the few minutes following the actual attending to the text. This is probably the most important part of listening instruction because it allows the learner to build mental representations. Post-listening tasks can involve additional reading, writing, speaking, and interaction.
- Encourage the use of active listening strategies. A successful listener is someone who adopts active listening strategies. An active listening strategy is an attempt to gain some control over the listening process.
- Build steps into activities that enhance language awareness. One goal of listening instruction is to help learners 'notice' more of the input and utilise more information from the input as they construct meaning.
- Reading comprehension should be considered as reading in another language and not merely an exercise in translation.

- Reading comprehension tasks comprise of a text surrounded by a number of tasks with the aim of closing the gap between the text and the reader.
- Reading and comprehension tasks need to include a number of components (pre-reading phase, while-reading phase and post-reading phase) to ensure that the interaction between text and reader is promoted.
- Developing writing is a key component in developing learners' ability to communicate in a second language. Communicative composing-oriented tasks can enhance writing skills, and provide L2 learners with various options about the content of what they can write.
- The task-based approach proposed in this chapter considers the various cognitive processes and principles responsible for developing writing skills:
  - Defining the rhetorical problem (goal/purpose and audience)
  - Planning (generating ideas, organising them, setting goals)
  - Reviewing (evaluation and review).
- Using communicative composing-oriented written tasks that engage learners in authentic and interactive writing activities is desirable. These types of tasks aim at improving learners' writing skills and consist of three phases:
  - Pre-writing phase
  - Writing phase
  - Focus on language phase.

What else can we read?

Brown, S. (2011) *Listening Myths*. University of Michigan Press.

Dave, W. and Willis, J. (2007) *Doing Task-based Teaching*. Oxford: Oxford University Press.

Ellis, R. (2003) *Task-based Language Learning and Teaching*. New York: Oxford University Press.

Grabe, W. (2009) *Reading in a Second Language: Moving from Theory to Practice*. New York: Cambridge University Press.

Field, J. (2008) *Listening in the Language Classroom*. Cambridge: Cambridge University Press.

Lee, J. (2000) *Tasks and Communicating in Language Classrooms*. New York: McGraw-Hill.

Nunan, D. (2004) *Task-based Language Teaching*. Cambridge: Cambridge University Press.

Polio, C. (2018) *Teaching Second Language Writing*. New York: Routledge.

Richards, J.C. (2012) *Tips for Teaching Listening*. London: Pearson.

Rost, M. (2002) *Teaching and Researching Listening. Applied Linguistics in Applied Linguistics in Action.* London: Longman.

Rost, M. and Wilson, J. (2013) *Active Listening*. London: Pearson.

Wilson, J.J. (2008) *How to Teach Listening*. Harlow: Pearson Longman.

Williams, J. (2005) *Teaching Writing in Second and Foreign Language Classrooms.* NJ: McGraw-Hill.

Zhao, H.H. and Anderson, N.J. (2009) *Second Language Reading Research and Instruction: Crossing the Boundaries*. Ann Arbor, MI: University of Michigan Press.

11 Language Tests

Can we take a minute to think about this?

Empirical research measuring the effects of instruction normally uses language tests. One of the problems with the empirical research on the effects of instruction is that there is a huge bias toward explicit testing (pencil and paper offline tests) and tapping of explicit knowledge in the research on the role of instruction. Future research needs to make use of inline testing (e.g. self-paced reading tests, eye-tracking tests) to measure the effects of instruction on the language implicit system and language processing.

However, no matter the type of testing, there are a number of guidelines that should be followed to develop a reliable and valid language test. Tests are an instrument used to collect data about the subjects' knowledge of a second language in areas such as vocabulary, grammar, language skills, metalinguistic awareness and general proficiency. Tests are considered dependent factors in second language research and are often used to measure the effects of an independent factor which is usually a teaching method or a teaching technique.

We must define linguistic and, more generally, communicative competence. Failure to do so, would lead to a number of misunderstandings.

What is the nature and role of language testing?

Different language tests measure different abilities or competences. Language tests can measure abilities such as: the ability to identify and remember new sounds; the ability to identify the grammatical functions of different parts of sentences; the ability to work out meanings without explanation in a new language; movement of the eyes during language processing; and many others.

As language instructors we must try to avoid creating negative reactions in the classroom testing we are involved in. We should always test for the best: give students the chance to demonstrate their optimal ability, to perform at their best.

Test writing is not and should not be a solitary activity. Other stakeholders will see problems with your tests that may have completely escaped your attention. They may interpret scoring procedures or items in a different way. They may find other errors that you cannot see because you are so close to the items having spent a long time constructing them.

Language tests need to be thoroughly evaluated before they are used. When you develop a language test the most important consideration is the use for which the test is intended, so its most important quality is its usefulness.

Test usefulness includes two main qualities: reliability, and validity.

Each of these qualities are complementary and test developers need to find a balance between them. This balance will vary from one testing situation to another.

Reliability

How do you understand reliability? What do you understand by a reliable test? Reliability can be defined as consistency of measurement, and is a measure of the degree to which a test gives the same results when it is given on different occasions or when it is used by different people.

Even if the scorers have been trained together and follow the same marking scheme, and even if no learning or forgetting has taken place, students will not behave in exactly the same way on every occasion. What we have to do is construct, administer and score each test in such a way that the scores actually obtained on a test on a particular occasion are likely to be very similar to those which would have been obtained if it had been set for the same students with the same ability, but at a different time. The more similar the scores would have been, the more reliable the test is said to be. Pre-testing is probably one of the answers.

Reliability is concerned with two components: the performance of test takers from occasion to occasion with the hope that the test is designed in such a way that test takers will perform in the same way if they take the test on two different occasions; and the reliability of the scoring.

All tests need to be thoroughly evaluated before they are used. The discussion of tasks and criteria for assessment is, in fact, a key contribution to achieve a valid and reliable testing procedure. Reliability can be defined as consistency of measurement and is a measure of the degree to which a test gives the same results when it is given on different occasions or when different people use it. Below is a list of Do's and Don'ts on how to make tests more reliable.

1. Take enough samples of behaviour. The more items you have in a test the more reliable the test will be. If you want to know how good an archer is, you don't rely on a single shot at the target. You want to see a large number of shots at the target. It is the same with language testing. The more items you give to the student taking the test, the more reliable the test will be.

2. Do not allow candidates too much freedom. The more freedom that is given, the greater the likelihood of a difference between the performance actually elicited and the performance that would have been elicited had the test be taken, say, a day later.

3. Write unambiguous items. What might be seen as unambiguous to the test setter might not make sense to the test taker. As we have said previously, in order to eliminate ambiguous items the test should be assessed by colleagues who should try very hard to find alternative interpretations to the one intended. Ensure that tests are well laid out and perfectly legible. Candidates should be familiar with format and testing techniques.

4. Provide uniform and non-distracting conditions of administration. Great care should be taken to ensure uniformity, in both timing and the acoustic test (listening test).

5. Provide a detailed scoring key. Specify acceptable responses and assign points for partially correct responses.

Validity

A test is said to be valid to the extent that it measures what it is supposed to measure. A test has content validity if its content constitutes a representative sample of the language skills and structures with which it is meant to be concerned. In an achievement test we will say that the test has content validity if the test refers to material covered in the teaching. A grammar test must be made for items testing knowledge or control of grammar. But this in itself does not ensure content validity. The test would have content validity only if it included a proper sample of the relevant structures. What the relevant structures are will depend upon the purpose of the test. Defining what we want to measure in a test is referred to as definition of construct. The evidence for construct validity is given here by the construct definition. You know exactly what you are measuring. You can add more evidence if you can demonstrate that the content of the test is representative of what has been covered during your instructional treatment period for example.

Language competence

Language competence is divided into hierarchical components of language knowledge, these components all interact with each other. It is this very interaction between knowledge and the language use context that characterises communicative language use. Language competence involves two components: language competence; and strategic competence. Language competence includes two broad categories: (i) organisational knowledge; and (ii) pragmatic knowledge.

(i)   Organisational knowledge is concerned with how the utterances or sentences and texts are organised. It comprises the abilities involved in controlling the formal structure of language for producing or recognising grammatically correct sentences, understanding their content and ordering them to form texts. It is divided into grammatical knowledge (how individual utterances or sentences are organised) and textual knowledge (how utterances or sentences are organised to form texts). Grammatical knowledge includes knowledge of vocabulary, syntax, phonology and graphology. Textual knowledge (how utterances or sentences are organised to form texts) is divided into two areas: knowledge of cohesion (relationship between sentences in written texts; use of conjunction, lexical cohesion, reference) and knowledge of rhetoric (how texts or conversations are organised).

(ii) Pragmatic knowledge relates utterances or sentences and texts to their meaning, to the intentions of language users (what does s/he really want to say?), and to the general characteristics of the language use setting (is it appropriate to say this like that in this context?). It is divided into two areas: functional knowledge and sociolinguistic knowledge. Functional knowledge enables us to

understand the relationship between utterances or sentences and texts and the intentions of language users. It is divided into:
- Knowledge of ideational functions: this enables us to express or interpret meaning in terms of our experience of the world.
- Knowledge of manipulative functions: this enables us to use language to influence the world around us – to get people to do things for us; to control what other people do; and to establish, maintain and change interpersonal relationships.
- Knowledge of heuristic functions: where we use language to extend our knowledge of the world around us.
- Knowledge of imaginative functions: jokes, use of figurative language, poetry.
- Sociolinguistic knowledge: this enables us to create or interpret language that is appropriate to a particular language use setting, e.g. writing a letter to a friend and writing a letter to a company for example. This includes knowledge of the dialect, registers, natural or idiomatic expressions, and cultural references and figures of speech.
- Strategic competence, which includes: goal setting (deciding what I am going to do); assessment (what do I need to complete this task? what do I have to work with?) and planning (how am I going to use what I know?).

Language ability has traditionally been considered to consist of four skills: listening, reading, speaking and writing. These four skills have traditionally been distinguished in terms of channels (audio and visual) and modes (productive and receptive).

What are the main points?

- Linguistic competence is a necessary requirement for somebody who wants to speak in another language. However, communicative competence is also necessary to be able to communicate competently in a second language. Communicative competence comprises the knowledge of the grammatical system of an L2 as well as the knowledge of the social and cultural contexts. Communicative language competence is made up of various components. Although it appears that language ability is divided into hierarchical components of language knowledge, these components all interact with each other and with features of the language use situation. It is the interaction between knowledge and language use in context that characterises communicative language use. Language competence involves two components: language knowledge and strategic competence.

- Language tests need to be thoroughly evaluated before they are used. When you develop a language test the most important consideration is the use for which the test is intended, so its most important quality is its usefulness. Test usefulness includes two main qualities: reliability, and validity.

What else can we read?

Brown, H.D. and Abeywickrama, P. (2010) *Language Assessment: Principles and Classroom Practices*. White Plains, NY: Pearson Education.

Bachman, L. and Palmer, A. (1996) *Language Testing in Practice*. Oxford: Oxford University Press.

Buck, G. (2001) *Assessing Listening*. Cambridge: Cambridge University Press.

Cho, Y. (2003) Assessing writing: Are we bound by only one method? *Assessing Writing*, 8: 165–91. https://doi.org/10.1016/s1075-2935(03)00018-7

Fulcher, G. (2013) *Practical Language Testing*. London: Routledge.

Green, A. (2013) *Exploring Language Assessment and Testing: Language in Action*. London: Routledge.

Read, J. (2013) Second language vocabulary assessment. *Language Teaching*, 46: 41–52. https://doi.org/10.1017/s0261444812000377

Taylor, L. (2011) *Examining Speaking: Research and Practice in Assessing Second Language Speaking*. Cambridge: Cambridge University Press.

12 Language Teaching Method

Can we take a minute to think about this?

One of the key questions that bothers language instructors is whether there is a particular method in language teaching better than others. Over the last many years, language teaching has been directly and indirectly influenced by theory and research in disciplines such as linguistics, education, psychology and second language acquisition. The principles derived from research have been translated in a number of teaching methods or language teaching approaches. From the grammar translation method through the audio-lingual method to the communicative language teaching approach. However, the lack of knowledge about the evidence behind a particular method or approach leads to the following misleading claims and a number of misunderstandings:

- The concept that there is a method or approach better than others.
- The fact that very often language instructors argue that a method and/or an approach is effective without any theoretical and empirical evidence to support this claim.
- Language can be learnt and taught explicitly.

What is the nature and role of a language teaching method?

The Grammar Translation Method is probably one of oldest teaching methods for language teaching used across many countries between the 1840s and 1940s. Originally it was used to teach Latin and Greek, and to help L2 learners to study foreign language literature. The main principle of this methodology was that L2 learners needed to develop the ability to read a text in another language and to translate that text from one language into another. Through the study of the grammar of the target language, the learner also became more familiar with the grammar of their mother tongue. The main goal for this method was to ensure that L2 learners attained high proficiency standards in translation and accuracy. The ability to communicate using the target language was not the main goal for language instruction.

The Direct Method was proposed as a reaction to the grammar translation method in terms of its approach to grammar teaching, vocabulary learning, teacher and learner's attitude, and language skills. While in the Grammar Translation Method the primary skills to improve were reading and writing, in the Direct Method the main emphasis was on listening and oral communication skills. In the Direct Method the role of the language teacher became more active. The teacher asked questions, engaged learners to participate in speaking activities and encouraged self-correction. L2 learners had to speak a lot as they were engaged in developing oral communicative skills.

The Direct Method was developed by Maximilian Berlitz at the turn of the 19th century and its principles were based on the attempt to make second language acquisition similar to first language acquisition. It was named 'direct' because meaning should be connected to the target language without translation into the native language. According to the Direct Method, language instructors should provide learners with opportunities to convey meaning through the use of the new language. L2 learners should use the target language without translating and without using their native language to communicate. The popularity of the Direct Method declined towards the beginning of the 1930s leading to the development of new methodologies in language teaching such as the Audio-Lingual Method.

In the late 1950s and the beginning of the 1960s, a new method in second language teaching, called the Audio-Lingual Method was developed. This method was underpinned by a second language acquisition theory called Behaviourism. The behaviourist's view was in strong opposition to Noam Chomsky's view of language and language acquisition that argued that humans have an innate language knowledge and that they are genetically programmed to develop their linguistic system in certain specific ways. Behaviourism maintained that it is the learners' experience which is largely responsible for language acquisition and this is more important that any innate capacity. This theory argued that the child's mind is a *tabula rasa*, and good language habits are learned through the process of repetition, imitation and reinforcement. According to this view second language acquisition is a progressive accumulation of habits and the ultimate goal is to produce language which is error-free. The first language was seen as a major obstacle to the acquisition of a second language since it caused interference errors (caused by habits in the L1) and negative transfer (from L1 to L2) of habits. It was believed that language acquisition proceeded from form to meaning, i.e. first master the grammatical forms and then move to express meaning. Supporters of this theory saw second language acquisition as a process of acquiring verbal habits. This theory was translated into the Audio-Lingual Method which emphasised the use of memorisation, mechanical and pattern drills practice.

In the late 1970s an innovative method called the Total Physical Response emerged. James Asher's Total Physical Response Method is a comprehension-based method to language teaching. The method assumes that language acquisition should start with understanding the language we hear or read before we proceed to production. It is a method of language teaching that makes use of physical movements to react to verbal input. The main characteristic of this method is that it focuses on meaning and comprehension. Verbal response is not necessary and students become performers. Verbal response is not necessary as the main focus is listening and acting.

The first comprehension-based approach to second language teaching was the so-called Natural Approach. It was developed by Tracy Terrell and supported by Stephen Krashen in the late 1970s early 1980s. This approach is based on the Monitor Theory developed by Stephen Krashen in the late 1970s. According to Stephen Krashen, there is a need for the creation of a kind of environment in the L2 classroom that resembles the condition where L1 learning takes place. He hypothesised that if L2 learners were exposed to 'comprehensible' input and were provided with opportunities to focus on meaning and messages rather than grammatical forms and accuracy, they would be able to acquire the L2 in much the same way as L1 learners acquire their first language. In order to maximise opportunities for comprehension experiences, language instructors create activities designed to teach students to recognise the meaning in words used in meaningful contexts, and to teach language learners to guess at the meaning of phrases without knowing all of the words and structures embedded in sentences or discourse. Language instructors must use visual aids (pictures, realia, gestures), modify their speech to aid comprehension, speak more slowly, emphasise key words, focus on simple and key vocabulary and grammar, use familiar topics and do not talk out of context.

A key development in language teaching was the emergence of the Communicative Language Teaching Approach. The main assumption behind this approach was that communicative language teaching programs will lead to the development of both Linguistic Competence (a knowledge of the rules of grammar) and Communicative Competence (a knowledge of the rules of language use). The development of a new communicative approach to language teaching is a complex one which is related to a number of disciplines. Noam Chomsky's criticism of Behaviourism, in undermining the credibility of the Audio-Lingual Method, sets the framework for a more child-centered approach which favours a highly inductive approach.

In the 1980s one could talk of a 'fever' for the Communicative Language Teaching Approach. Communicative Language Teaching was considered to be a type of instruction, an approach to language teaching rather than a method. It was the growing discontent on the part of language teachers with the previous methods, together with the need for a new method that led methodologists to find a way which would essentially bring the learner into closer contact with the target language community. Communicative Language Teaching makes us consider language not only in terms of its structures but also in terms of the communicative functions that it performs. Therefore, this approach aims at understanding what people do with language forms when they communicate. The Communicative Language Teaching Approach is a student-centred type of instruction, a very revolutionary approach to language teaching as it considers findings from both language teaching, and second language acquisition theory and empirical research.

If the language classroom can become an area of co-operative negotiation, joint interpretation, and the sharing of expression, then the language teacher is in the position to give the students the opportunity for spontaneous, unpredictable exploratory production of language when involved in classroom language tasks.

The main contribution of this new type of instruction is the shift from attention to the grammatical forms to the communicative properties of the language. The language instructor creates the opportunity and the conditions in the classroom for learners to interact in a communicative way. This is to say that the L2 learner has someone to talk to, something to talk about, and a desire to understand and to make himself/herself understood.

If that happens, language acquisition can take place naturally and teaching can be extremely effective.

The Communicative Language Teaching Approach was in direct antithesis with the Presentation– Production–Practice-model (PPP). The practice stage in PPP aimed to provide opportunities for L2 learners to use the grammatical properties of the target language. Criticism of this model suggested that the practice stage was not conducive to communication. Forcing learners to use certain structures in a practice activity does not necessarily mean language learners will use these structures spontaneously later in their speech.

CLIL stands for Content and Language Integrated Learning. In a nutshell, it is the teaching of subjects to learners through the use of the target language. For example, the teacher will teach drama to a class of ESL students from Japan. Subject matter and target language are therefore integrated and taught at once. This dual approach has two main aims: (a) one related to a particular subject; and (b) one related to language. If you are teaching Italian you can use as a subject matter 'history of art'.

The teaching is organised around the content of information that learners will acquire and not around the linguistic characteristics of the language. Subject matter content is used for teaching purposes and language instructors need to provide learners with assistance in understanding subject matter texts. Learners become highly motivated and are exposed to authentic material and tasks. Language is used to convey specific content. This approach is built on the principles of the Communicative Language Teaching Approach and therefore it emphasises the importance of real and meaningful communication where information is exchanged between interlocutors.

Task-Based Language Teaching initially became popular in the 1990s. It referred to a type of language teaching which takes 'tasks' as its key units for designing and implementing language instruction. The main principles of Task-Based Language Teaching approach are:

- Learners should be provided with opportunities to make the language input they receive more comprehensible;
- Learners should be engaged in contexts in which they need to produce output which others can understand;
- Learners should be exposed to real-life language situations in the language classroom.

Task-Based Language Teaching aims at providing L2 learners with a natural context to use the target language. The goal of this approach is twofold: to promote implicit knowledge as a result of the effort to communicate; to develop fluency by attempting to use the L2 in real operating conditions. Learners work to complete a task and have plenty of opportunities for interaction and negotiation of meaning as they have to understand each other and express their own meaning. Task-Based Language Teaching aims at integrating all four language skills and providing opportunities for the learners to experiment with and explore both spoken and written language through learning activities which are designed to engage L2 learners in the authentic, practical and functional use of language for meaningful purposes (i.e. to cultivate the learners' communicative competence).

What are the main points?

The Grammar Translation Method focuses on developing L2 learners' ability to read a text in another language and to translate that text from one language into another. The Direct Method focuses on providing L2 learners with the opportunity to use the target language to express meaning. The Audio-Lingual Method makes use of memorisation and mechanical and pattern drills practice to develop L2 learners' language skills. The Total Physical Response Method focuses on developing practices that initially improve L2 learners' ability in listening and reading before speaking and writing skills. The Natural Approach argues that L2 learners should be exposed to comprehensible and message-oriented input, and that language teaching should not be built around grammatical or vocabulary units but instead themes or topics. The Communicative Language Teaching Approach represents a philosophy of teaching that is based on communicative language use. It emphasises notional–functional concepts and communicative competence, rather than grammatical structures, as central to language teaching. The Content and Language Integrated Learning is an approach in language education designed to provide L2 learners with instruction in content and language. Task-Based Language Teaching focuses on asking students to undertake meaningful tasks using the target language.

Over the last 80 years a variety of methods (e.g. Grammar-Translation, Audio-Lingual Method) and approaches (e.g. Natural Approach, Communicative Language Teaching, Task-Based Language Teaching) have been proposed for the teaching of languages. Language teachers have been interested in finding innovative and more effective ways to teach languages. In order to provide teachers with effective options for language teaching, we should consider carefully what we know about how a language is acquired.

An effective approach to language teaching is one based on, and informed by, theory and empirical research in second language acquisition. Although research in second language acquisition mainly focuses on learners and learning, the findings from this research have very often implications for language teachers and teaching. In the next chapter, some of the key and relevant questions addressed in second language acquisition research will be examined. The implications of this research for language teaching will be highlighted in order to provide effective options for language teaching and teachers and to work towards a more principled and evidence-based approach to language teaching.

- Teaching communicatively means having a good working definition of communication. Communication can be defined as the expression, interpretation and negotiation of meaning for a specific purpose in a given context: to produce language for the purpose of expressing meaning.
- Language is too abstract and complex to teach and learn explicitly. A focus on form should be input-oriented and meaning based (e.g. textual enhancement, input flood and structured input). Move from input to output practice.
- Instructors and materials should provide student learners with level-appropriate input and interaction. Meaningful and comprehensible input must be integrated in language teaching.
- Tasks (and not exercises or activities) should form the backbone of the curriculum.
- Instructors should provide indirect and implicit corrective feedback.

What else can we read?

Benati, A. (2020) *Key Questions in Language Teaching: An Introduction.* Cambridge: Cambridge University Press.

Asher, J. (1977) *Learning Another Language Through Actions: The Complete Teacher's Guide Book.* Los Gatos, CA: Sky Oaks Productions.

Hinkel, E. (2005) *Handbook of Research in Second Language Teaching and Learning.* Mahwah, NJ: Lawrence Erlbaum Associates.

Krashen, S. and Terrell, T. (1983) *The Natural Approach: Language Acquisition in the Classroom.* Hayward, CA: Alemany Press.

Long, M. and Doughty, C. (2009) *The Handbook of Language Teaching.* Oxford: Wiley-Blackwell.

Long, H.M. (2018) A micro process-product study of CLIL lesson: Linguistic modifications, content dilution and vocabulary knowledge. *Instructed Second Language Acquisition*, 2: 3–38. https://doi.org/10.1558/isla.33605

Richards, J.C. and Rodgers, T.S. (2001) *Approaches and Methods in Language Teaching.* Cambridge: Cambridge University Press.

Schwieter, J. and Benati, A. (2019) *The Cambridge Handbook of Language Learning.* Cambridge: Cambridge University Press.

13 Learning and Acquisition

(with Víctor Parra-Guinaldo)

Can we take a minute to think about this?

Some scholars and researchers argue that language is like any other complex mental task such as reading, playing chess and, in general, solving problems. Like any other complex mental phenomenon it is learned via the same domain-general mechanisms that enable us to learn how to program a computer or solve difficult puzzles.

Language is special and it *is not* learned in the same way as other complex mental phenomena. Humans are hardwired to learn language and have special cognitive mechanisms specifically designed to deal with language. These are separate mechanisms from the domain-general one.

The distinction made here sheds some light on the misleading views about second language acquisition highlighted below.

- Language is learned like any other skill.
- Practising language makes perfect.
- The learning system turns into the acquisition system (explicit knowledge turns into implicit knowledge).
- Individual factors, such as motivation, play a role in second language acquisition.

What is the nature and role of learning and acquisition?

The study of second language acquisition is the study of how L2 learners come to create a new language system with often a limited exposure to the second language. It is the study of how they can make use of that system during comprehension and speech production. For the purpose of clarification, a second language (L2) refers to a language that it is acquired after the first language (L1) has been established in early childhood. Theory and research in second language acquisition has emphasised the complexity of acquisition processes. How learners process language, how they intake it and accommodate it into the new language system, and how they access the information for speech production, are key areas of research in this field.

Second language acquisition is a complex phenomenon as it entails the acquisition of different systems (e.g. the phonological system, the lexical system, the morphological system, the syntactical system, etc.). It also consists of a number of mechanisms/processes which are responsible for how L2 learners are able to process (input) the characteristics of the new language and eventually use the language for language production (output). The field of second language acquisition addresses two fundamental questions:

(a) How do L2 learners come to internalise the linguistic system of another language?
(b) How do L2 learners make use of that linguistic system during comprehension and speech production?

Language acquisition has been viewed as a progressive accumulation of habits with the ultimate goal of error-free production. The L1 was seen as a major obstacle to L2 acquisition since it caused interference errors (caused by habits in the L1) and negative transfer (from L1 to L2) of habits. The concept of positive and negative transfer was central to Behaviourism. Positive transfer is when learners transfer a structure that is appropriate and similar in both languages. Negative transfer is when learners use inappropriately a L1 structure in the L2. The easiest L2 structures to learn are the ones which exists in learners' L1 and have the same form and meaning. For example, a Spanish speaker translating 'el libro de Juan' into English as 'the book of John' instead of 'John's book' would be a case of negative transfer. Interestingly though, this could turn into a case of positive transfer if 'The Book of John' is understood in the Biblical sense. In this last sense, possession is expressed analytically, like in Spanish (by means of a preposition), whereas in 'John's book' possession is expressed synthetically (by adding the ending 's). Within the behaviourist framework, theorists believe that language acquisition involves acquiring verbal habit formation. Learners proceed from form to meaning, i.e. first master the grammatical forms and then move on to express meaning. Certain conditions are applied for acquiring these habits:

1   The learner imitates and repeats the language heard.
2   The imitation has to be rewarded.
3   As a result of this, the behaviour is reinforced and eventually becomes habitual.

The universal grammar (UG) theoretical framework claims of this theory is that it sees languages as a complex and abstract system which develops in the human mind. Noam Chomsky argued that all humans possess innate knowledge of language universals and principles which regulate the acquisition of languages. These principles restrict the type of grammar that can be attained; in other words, UG tells us what is possible and what is not in grammar. Meanwhile, there are parameters that determine what needs to be fixed or modified in each particular grammar (or language) in light of the input the speaker is exposed to. For example, the combination of subject (S) and verb (V) to form a simple sentence is a principle of UG that all languages possess, but whether S should precede V or vice versa is determined by the parameter of each language, as the case may be. English has an S+V order, whereas the most typical word order for the Celtic languages for example is V+S. Researchers within this theoretical framework have been concerned with how languages are represented in the mind (mental representation of language) and how learners come to know more about a language than what they have been exposed to. L2 learners make projections about the language they learn which is often beyond the information they are supposed to know (poverty of the stimulus). In other words, they sometime know how a linguistic feature works, what is grammatical or ungrammatical without having been exposed to that particular feature.

L2 learners have their own internal syllabus (abstract principles) to follow which constrains language acquisition. The information contained in our mind (innate universal grammar system) influences the development of a second language (internal system). When learners are exposed to input, that input resets their internal abstract principles by means of parameters specific to each language. For example, L1 English learners would need to modify the parameter that language is 'head initial' (*Alessandro speaks Japanese*) to the parameter of 'head final' when learning Japanese (*Alessandro Japanese speaks* or *Japanese Alessandro speaks*). All humans have universal features of language which constrain the acquisition of grammar and parameters which tell us in what way we apply those principles. To use a metaphor, electricity could be considered a universal principle, but each language would have a parameter determining whether to leave the light switch on or off. Likewise, the existence of a head (H) is a universal principle, but whether 'head first' is switched on or off is determined by the 'head parameter' in each language. In general, English is considered a 'head first' language, so the 'head first parameter' would be switched on, whereas Japanese is considered 'head final' (not 'head first') and therefore the 'head first parameter' would be switched off. Consequently, switching a parameter on or off is a much simpler operation than having two separate rules, one for 'head first' and one for 'head final'. This is important in generative grammar, because its main goal is to explain the poverty of stimulus conundrum; in other words, a simplified mechanism of acquisition helps us to understand how a child is able to acquire such a complex system with such an impoverished input in such a short period of time. Children are able to acquire rules (subconsciously, that is) even when their parents may make mistakes or their speech is impaired by, say, hesitation or interruption.

The truth of the matter is that L2 learners acquire language mainly through exposure to comprehensible input in a similar fashion to how they acquire their first language. The main pre-requisite for this to happen is that learners are exposed to comprehensible and message-oriented input. It is paramount that L2 learners are exposed to input (comprehensible) which is slightly above their proficiency level (i+1) and learn a second language in a very relaxed environment.

When L2 learners acquire a second language they develop two systems that are independent from each other. The 'acquisition system' (unconscious and implicit) is activated when we are engaged in communication. The 'learning system' (conscious and explicit) functions as a monitor and corrector of our production.

What are the main points?

Acquisition is a term normally associated with the internalisation of the linguistic system. Distinctions have been made between learning and acquisition:

- Learning refers to the conscious process of learning the grammatical rules of a target language from a textbook and/or instruction.

> This results in a particular kind of knowledge system called the 'explicit' system.

- Acquisition instead involves processes by which L2 learners internalise language from exposure to the language input they are exposed to. Acquisition takes place because L2 learners are exposed to input, not because instructors teach L2 learners a rule or because he or she practises it. Acquisition results in an implicit (unconscious) linguistic system, similar to L1 system.

- L2 learners are limited in what they can do with explicit information, that ultimately communication involves tapping into the acquired linguistic system and not the learned linguistic system. The learned system can be used for monitoring.

- Learning and acquisition are separate processes that result in separate systems that do not interact. Most importantly, learning cannot become acquisition. That is, one doesn't learn rules and through practice acquire them. Acquisition happens only through exposure to comprehensible and meaningful input.

We should emphasise that today, regardless of distinctions we can make between learning vs. acquisition, we accept that L2 learners develop an implicit mental representation of language. At the same time, it is accepted that L2 learners might also develop explicit learned knowledge. There is no evidence to demonstrate the learned system turn into the acquired system.

What else can we read?

Gass, S. and Selinker, L. (2008) *Second Language Acquisition. An Introductory Course*. New York: Routledge.

Herschensohn, J. and Young-Scholten, M. (2013) *The Cambridge Handbook of Second Language Acquisition*. Cambridge: Cambridge University Press.

Hummel, K.M. (2014) *Introducing Second Language Acquisition. Perspectives and Practices*. Chichester: John Wiley & Sons.

Ortega, L. (2008) *Understanding Second Language Acquisition*. Oxford: Oxford University Press.

VanPatten, B. and Williams, J. (2007) *Theories in Second Language Acquisition*. Mahwah, NJ: Lawrence Erlbaum Associates.

14 L1 and L2 Acquisition

Can we take a minute to think about this?

One of the key questions in second language acquisition is whether or know learning a first language is similar or different to learning a second language. Very often the lack of knowledge about L1 and L2 acquisition processes leads to misleading claims and misunderstandings. To address these we need to consider two issues:

- The role of innate knowledge.
- The two main hypotheses about possible differences and similarities between L1 and L2 acquisition.

To develop the right understanding about L1 and L2 acquisition has implications for our understanding about learning a language, and pedagogical implications on how we should teach languages to facilitate acquisition.

What is the role of innate knowledge?

One of the key issues in language learning is to establish what (if anything) learners bring with them when they learn a language. Under normal conditions, all children acquire their first language without much effort and no formal instruction. It has been argued that one of the reasons for this is that they have a mechanism (language acquisition device) that guides them in the acquisition of their first language.

This mechanism consists of general innate principles about language, and it is applicable and common to all languages. When learning a language, the samples of the language to which children have been exposed serve as the trigger needed for the activation of those principles and prevent the children from making the wrong hypotheses about the acquisition of their first language. This innate abstract knowledge allows children to discover the rules of their L1 language system without any delays. Children successfully learn their native language/s at a time in life when they would not be expected to learn anything else so cognitively complicated. They all achieve mastery of the structure of the spoken language spoken and know language rules and patterns that they have not been exposed to previously. They acquire their first language successfully even when they do not receive feedback or formal instruction.

The question is: how come learners find it extremely difficult to learn and master a second language? Do we have access to this innate knowledge, these principles, when we learn a second language? There are three possible views in regard to access to innate knowledge:

(a) L2 acquisition is different from L1 acquisition and it is not constrained by this innate knowledge. Internal universal principles about language are not responsible for L2 acquisition and the acquisition process is generally seen as a problem-solving one.

(b) L2 acquisition is constrained by this innate knowledge, and L2 learners still have access to those internal principles governing language. L1 and L2 acquisition are similar.

(c) L2 learners transfer to the learning of the second language a limited portion of their L1, perhaps something from the lexicon and its properties, but might not carry across other features (e.g. functional, syntax) which are constrained by the internal universal principles.

Scholars, in support of the difference between L1 and L2 acquisition, argue that the acquisition processes of children and adults differ fundamentally in terms of the presence or absence of 'innate ability'. Children possess this innate knowledge which positively affects the speed and accuracy of L1 language acquisition. Adults don't possess it any longer, and they result to using problem-solving skills and conscious attention to acquire an L2. Success might depend on how well those problem-solving skills are deployed. L2 learners use their L1 knowledge (transfer) to develop their L2 language. A number of characteristics distinguish L2 from L1 acquisition: (a) lack of success; (b) role of affective factors such as motivation; (c) correlation to age.

What are the similarities and differences between L1 and L2 acquisition?

The issue as to whether L1 and L2 acquisition are similar or different is the underlying question of all the many others raised in this field of research. Two of the key questions generated from this line of research are: (a) To what extent first language (L1) and second language (L2) acquisition are similar or different; (b) To what extent learners transfer the L1 system into the new L2 system.

Scholars have investigated the nature of L1 and L2 and, overall, their findings have indicated that there are similarities and some differences between L1 and L2 acquisition. In the development of both L1 and L2, learners need input to develop a language internal system. Input is the main ingredient for success in both L1 and L2 acquisition. Good language input must have two requisites: (a) language learners must comprehend it; and (b) it must contain a message and have a message-oriented input. So, the first question is: (a) to what extent are first language (L1) and second language (L2) acquisition similar or different?

Similarities

1. In both the L1 and L2 acquisition, learners follow predictable stages and natural orders in the acquisition of formal features of the target language. Findings from research have indicated that there is a specific and similar order in the acquisition of grammatical morphemes such as inflectional features, in all languages. For example, past tense inflection -ed- is acquired before third person singular -s-.
2. L1 and L2 acquisition require extensive exposure of comprehensible and meaningful input.
3. L1 and L2 acquisition are fundamentally similar in terms of internal processes and mechanisms responsible for language acquisition. Potential differences between L1 and L2 acquisition can be attributed to external factors such as availability and type of exposure to language input and interaction. Children are consistently exposed to a good quantity and quality of simplified input. Adults don't have the same opportunity.

Differences

1   In acquiring the L1, children might have full access to the innate and internal language principles. Adults, on the other hand, might not have access to the same innate ability when learning the L2, and therefore they might resort to using problem-solving skills to acquire the target language.
2   Adults are not exposed to the same quantity and quality of input.
3   The difference in context of L1 and L2 acquisition plays an important role. While it is possible to acquire an L2 in various contexts, L1 acquisition takes place only in a natural context and in the social group in which the child is growing up. In this context, the child gets good quality L1 input.

The second question is: (b) to what extent do learners transfer the L1 system into the new L2 system?

The role of L1 transfer is still very much debated in second language acquisition. However, the debate has moved away from the idea that learners automatically transfer the L1 into the L2 and errors are simply the results of L1 interference.

Current findings from research have demonstrated the following:

- L1 does not seem to influence acquisition orders and sequences. No matter the L1 of the learner, L2 learners seem to go through similar orders and stages in acquiring grammatical forms and structures (e.g. *-ing* is processed before *-ed*).
- L1 does not seem to be the main cause of learners' errors in L2. For example, English native speakers can use L1 speech procedures to cope with L2 production (they say *sono venti anni* instead of *ho venti anni* – I am twenty years old instead of I have twenty years old). This type of error is a communicative strategy used by L2 learners (English native speakers learning Italian) to produce a sentence by dressing up their own L1 utterance in L2 vocabulary. There are more complex linguistics and cognitive constraints and processes responsible for learners' errors.
- L1 transfer is constrained by universal aspects of language and internal language processing. For instance, L2 learners make use

of implicit and universal processing strategies when they process grammar in the input.

What are the main points?

- Overall, to a certain extent, L1 and L2 acquisition share the same processes and mechanisms for the development of an internal language system.
- The difference in context of L1 and L2 acquisition plays an important role in the acquisition process. While it is possible to learn an L2 in various contexts, L1 acquisition takes place only in a natural context and in the social group in which the child is growing up and where the child gets L1 input only.
- Difference between L1 and L2 can be attributed to external factors (e.g. quality and quantity of input) and not internal processes.
- First and second language acquisition require the same ingredient to be successful: comprehensible and message-oriented input.
- First and second language acquisition require language learners to engage in contexts in which they hear and see language in communicative settings and they engage in comprehension and interaction with that input.
- First and second language acquisition have both ordered language development. The same factors seem to impact development: universals of language, frequency in the input, among others.
- First and second language acquisition are not responsive to outside manipulation. The effects of instruction on language development are limited, and in some cases non-existent.
- First and second language acquisition are affected by both input and interaction. In both contexts, being part of communicative interactions gets the learner a more appropriate level of input.
- First and second language acquisition are both mainly implicit. Explicit learning may serve more of an affective factor. Mental representation is far more complex, and more abstract than any explicit learning or processing could achieve. Implicit processing and organisation of linguistics are key factors in language development.

- Second language learners have something internal to them that first language learners do not: another language (or other languages). However, the influence of the first language is constrained by the universals of language. The presence or absence of another language in the mind/brain does not obviate the role of input and does not compromise ordered language development. So, the presence of the first language inside the mind/brain of language learners does not alter the processes or block what the internal mechanisms responsible for language development do or must do.

What else can we read?

Birdsong, D. and Paik, J. (2008) Second language acquisition and ultimate attainment. In Spolsky, B. and Hult, F. (eds), *Handbook of Educational Linguistics* (424–36). Oxford: Blackwell.

Bley-Vroman, R. (2009) The evolving context of the Fundamental Difference Hypothesis. *Studies in Second Language Acquisition*, 31: 175–98. https://doi.org/10.1017/s0272263109090275

Clahsen, H. and Felser, C. (2006) How native-like is non-native language processing? *Trends in Cognitive Sciences*, 10: 564–70. https://doi.org/10.1016/j.tics.2006.10.002

De Angelis, G. (2007) *Third or Additional Language Acquisition*. Clevedon: Multilingual Matters.

DeKeyser, R. (2015) Skill Acquisition Theory. In VanPatten, B. and Williams, J. (eds), *Theories in Second Language Acquisition* (94–112). New York: Routledge.

Pienemann, M. and Lenzing, A. (2015) Processability theory. In VanPatten, B. and Williams, J. (eds), *Theories in Second Language Acquisition* (159–79). New York: Routledge.

Schwieter, J.W. (2015) *The Cambridge Handbook of Bilingual Processing*. Cambridge: Cambridge University Press.

Ullman, M. (2001) The declarative/procedural model of lexicon and grammar. *Journal of Psycholinguistic Research*, 30: 37–69. https://doi.org/10.1023/A:1005204207369

VanPatten, B. and Benati, A. (2010) *Key Terms in Second Language Acquisition*. London: Continuum.

Vetter, E. (2012) Multilingualism pedagogy: building bridges between languages. In Hüttner, J., Schiftner, B., Mehlmauer, B. and Reichl, S. (eds), *Theory and Practice in EFL Teacher Education. Bridging the Gap* (228–46). Bristol: Multilingual Matters.

White, L. (2003) *Second Language Acquisition and Universal Grammar*. Cambridge: Cambridge University Press.

15 Motivation

Can we take a minute to think about this?

There is no doubt that motivation is one of the key components of all our endeavours in life. Humans strongly believe that without motivation we might not be able to get very far in life. The question is: can motivation be a good predictor of how far people get in language acquisition? Assuming that this is the case, it would lead to some misleading claims. One existing belief is that motivation is a key factor in the acquisition of a second language. The more motivated a person is, the more the chances that he/she will acquire a second language. To avoid any misunderstanding and misconceptions about motivation, we need to keep in mind the following:

- Language is not a skill. Acquiring a language is not like any other learning in life such as playing tennis or learning how to drive a car. Language acquisition is a complex, abstract and implicit process.
- Deriving from that assumption about language is the fact that motivation can't tell us very much about how second language acquisition happens, or explain the various linguistic and processing constraints involved in acquisition. Motivation does not have the power to explain the process involved in second language acquisition.

What is the nature and role of motivation?

Motivation is another individual difference that has received a good deal of attention and has also undergone evolution as a construct. Basically, motivation refers to a willingness to learn or do something. However, within SLA we have seen motivation move from a static construct related to socio-psychological variables (e.g. how the learner perceives the target language and culture, and the degree to which the learner wishes to interact with the latter) to more cognitive-oriented constructs (e.g. the mental self of learners), to constructs related to contemporary psychology on self-esteem, self-regulation, and other advances in research on human personality. Ultimately, all are related to *desire*. The reason for such shifts in scholarly attention is that researchers are trying to uncover the sources of motivation vis à vis learner internal factors. It is widely held that motivation, no matter where it comes from or how it works, is somehow related to successful acquisition, much as it is related to successful dieting or successful completion of a book. In short, motivated people stick with tasks. This is important in SLA because SLA is such a protracted process; it takes years for someone to reach advanced levels of ability with language.

L2 researchers have discussed two distinct motivations in the SLA context: *integrative* and *instrumental*. (i) Integrative motivation refers to the internal impetus that learners have to relate to, identify with, or perhaps otherwise 'integrate' into another L2 culture. It involves the psychological and emotional dimensions of how people construct identity and how they interact with others. (ii) Instrumental motivation is related to purposeful use of language, such as wanting language for educational, economic, or other benefits. With this kind of motivation, language is seen as a tool to get goods, to derive benefits from the environment that are not psychological in nature (even though we might feel good after we derive the benefit).

The field of motivation research has become more complicated to include such things as the possible and ideal selves, motivation as process, demotivation, the evolution of motivation over time, among other concepts.

What are the main points?

- Motivation is one of a number of what researchers call individual differences (traits that vary across individuals). Motivation to learn another language is, simply conceived, the degree and type of 'wanting to learn' and has been shown to correlate significantly with how far learners get (e.g. how much language they acquire, the skills they develop with the language).
- The main question that research on individual differences addresses is this: what is the relationship, if any, between individual differences and ultimate attainment or success? Many second lan-

guage researchers have assumed that individual differences, such as motivation, play an important role in determining outcomes for L2 learners. Research on individual differences may help explain why some language learners might acquire more of the second language compared to other learners. However, research on individual differences fails to explain two key things:

(a) how language gets into our head;
(b) what language gets into our head.

- Motivation does not affect the underlying processes of acquisition. It does not affect ordered development, the role of input, the role of the L1, the role of universals and universal grammar.

What else can we read?

Dornyei, Z. (2001) *Motivational Strategies in the Language Classroom.* Cambridge: Cambridge University Press.

Dornyei, Z. (2001) *Teaching and Researching Motivation.* Harlow: Longman.

Dornyei, Z. (2005) *The Psychology of the Language Learner: Individual Differences in Second Language Acquisition.* Mahwah, NJ: Lawrence Erlbaum Associates.

VanPatten, B. (2003) *From Input to Output: A Teacher's Guide to Second Language Acquisition.* New York: McGraw-Hill.

16 Output

Can we take a minute to think about this?

Output refers to the language that L2 learners produce in communicative contexts. It is language learners use to express their own meaning. For output to have a communicative purpose, it must be linked to specific intents, and the meaning of the language produced must be central to the task (e.g. making a grocery list, planning a holiday, attending an interview and talking about your education and experience, etc.).

There is a clear misconception about the role of output in language teaching: you have to speak in order to learn a language. The idea is that you can't learn Chinese or French unless you practise speaking these languages. What does the research tell us about this position? The view that L2 learners should be asked to produce language too prematurely is the result of a series of misunderstandings and misleading claims around the role of output in second language acquisition.

The kind of output practice often used by instructors in the language classroom *is not* language that L2 learners would produce in communicative contexts. Learners are asked to repeat a sentence, transform a sentence (e.g. present tense sentence into the past tense), or engage in practice where the focus is grammar (e.g. tell me your daily routine to practise reflexive verbs in Italian, or tell me what you did last night to practise basic present tense, etc.). Output as part of interaction is not merely practice but communication with a purpose. In output as part of meaningful interaction, learners do not use language for the sake of using language. They use language to get something done or to let someone know something.

One of the key questions around the role of output is: is output necessary for second language acquisition? Is input enough for developing the ability to use language in a communicative context?

What is the nature and role of output?

Output refers to the language learners' need to produce in order to express meaning in a classroom dynamic in which language instructors and L2 learners take new roles and responsibilities. Output is generally defined as any attempt by an L2 learner to produce language in spoken, written, or signed forms. When learners produce output, they are not engaged in comprehension as they are with input.

As we know, comprehensible and message-oriented input and interactions play key roles in the acquisition of a second language. Output practice should help L2 learners to use the target language for a specific purpose and intent and should not be just mechanical practice.

What is the role of output? Output does not play the same role as input. It does not provide the raw material (as input) for the development of L2 learners' implicit system. Most perspectives in second language research do not hold that communicatively embedded output is necessary for second language acquisition. The one exception is the skill theory where the main concern is not what grows in the mind/brain of the learner but instead how particular abilities deploy language in real time (skill development). How knowledge can become the ability to use the language automatically for the purpose of speaking. At the extreme end of this perspective is the view that output plays no role in the acquisition of language.

There is clear support for the view that output can facilitate the development of language skill. Skill is the ability of learners to use language fluently. The idea that output might have a beneficial role in language acquisition comes from studies of French immersion programs in Canada. Native English speakers in these programs, despite the abundant comprehensible input received, failed to acquire full grammatical competence in the target language. In particular, although learners had good receptive skills (listening and reading skills), their production was marked by persistent non-target like forms, especially when it came to morphological marking.

The main explanation of these findings was that L2 learners were not being pushed to produce language output. Although output does not have the same key role as input, it may have beneficial effects on L2 learners' development.

The so-called pushed output might have a beneficial role in second language acquisition.

NNS: And in hand in hand have a bigger glass to see.
NS: It' err. You mean, something in his hand?
NNS: Like spectacle. For older person.
NS: Mmmm, sorry I don't follow, it's what?
NNS: In hand have he have has a glass for looking through for make
the print bigger to see, to see the print, for magnify.
NS: He has some glasses?
NNS: Magnify glasses he has magnifying glasses.
NS: Oh aha I see a magnifying glass, right that's a good one, ok.

Pushed output refers to speech or writing that forces L2 learners to produce language correctly, precisely, and appropriately. Producing target language might trigger learners to pay attention to the language needs and convey their own intended meanings in speech production. Output may stimulate learners to move from semantic, open-ended, non-deterministic, strategic processing prevalent in comprehension to the complete grammatical processing needed for accurate production.

Output might have the following beneficial roles:

- Output might help learners to improve fluency.
- Output might help learners to notice a gap.
- Output might trigger input modifications.
- Output might help learners to test hypotheses.

Output creates greater automaticity and helps to develop fluency in L2 learners. The more you practise, the more automatic a skill becomes. Little effort is required to execute an automatic process involved when the learner carries out an activity which requires them to complete a task without awareness or attention. It becomes routinised and automatised just as the steps involved in walking towards a bike, getting out the key, unlocking it, pushing it, getting on it and riding it, require little thought.

Output (oral and written) might help L2 learners to consolidate and to modify their existing linguistic knowledge. A possible beneficial function for output is to push L2 learners to notice existing gaps in their linguistic knowledge. Output can be seen as an opportunity for learners to 'notice' the gap between what they want to say and what they can actually say when interacting with others. As L2 learners are trying to make their speech comprehensible, they might become more aware of what they still need to learn about the target language and become more receptive to certain structures/forms in the input. Producing speech might draw learners' attention to form and structures they need to learn.

Output in the form of interaction with other interlocutors might also have beneficial effects. The structure of the interaction between speakers can be modified and these modifications, called negotiation of meaning, can facilitate acquisition. Negotiation of meaning refers to the efforts, including comprehension checks, confirmation checks and clarification requests, that native and non-native speakers make to modify or restructure the interaction in order to overcome difficulties in comprehension. One outcome of negotiating meaning is that learner output may trigger better input from other speakers. These discourse strategies provide L2 learners with input adequately suited to their development needs. Output causes changes in the input learners receive, and this has a direct effect on learner development. Interacting with others is about getting qualitatively better input. In other words, interaction gets learners more comprehensible, or communicatively embedded, modified input.

Output might help L2 learners to test hypotheses. For example, if they are not sure about the use of a form they might try out sentences with another speaker (native speaker) and/or receive some feedback. This feedback refers to the incorrectness of their utterances from an interlocutor (e.g. confirmation checks, recast) when learners produce output. In this way L2 learners might proceed to test a hypothesis about what the correct form is or ask the other speaker for the word. The feedback received by L2 learners about the fact that they are doing 'something wrong' should help them to pay attention to the input in order to modify their output. In this case, feedback might positively stimulate learners' attention.

Scholars in this field agree that input is a necessary element in second language acquisition. Output has a different role to input, but might have a facilitative role in developing a skill. Existing empirical evidence seems to suggest that output, especially as part of interaction, may facilitate the acquisition of certain features (e.g. lexical items, verb inflections). However, current empirical evidence has not demonstrated that output and interaction assist in the development of syntax, for example.

What are the main points?

- While we accept that input is indispensable for acquisition, output might have a facilitative role. Output, as part of interaction, may enhance acquisition. However, the research has yet to convincingly demonstrate that output and interaction assist in the development of formal features of the language related to syntax and there is no evidence that it plays any significant role in the properties of language governed by universal grammar. There is evidence that interaction may facilitate the acquisition of lexical items (words) and their meanings, and there is also evidence that it may promote acquisition of certain transparent surface features of language such as certain verb and noun inflections.

- Interaction can be linked to the development of skill (speaking) and to the development of lexicon and surface features of language. However, it cannot be linked to the development of competence or a mental representation of language.

What else can we read?

DeKeyser, R.M. (2007) *Practice in a Second Language. Perspectives from Applied Linguistics and Cognitive Psychology*. Cambridge: Cambridge University Press.

Pienemann, M. (1998) *Language Processing and L2 Development*. Amsterdam: John Benjamins.

Swain, M. (1995) Three functions of output in second language learning. In Cook, G. and Seidlhofer, B. (eds), *Principles and Practice in Applied Linguistics* (125–44). Oxford: Oxford University Press.

VanPatten, B. (2003) *From Input to Output*. NJ: McGraw-Hill.

17 The Role of the Instructor and the Learner

Can we take a minute to think about this?

The role of the language instructor and the learner in the language class-room has changed considerably over the years. The traditional view was based on the assumption that the language instructor possesses all the knowledge about the language and this is transmitted to the learner. The role of the learner then becomes one of the *note-taker* and the *parrot* who repeats the language heard from the language instructor. Along with this view is the wrong belief that repetition and imitation are key components for successful language acquisition.

These misconceptions and misleading claims have serious consequences on language learning and teaching:

- Lack of opportunities for exposure to meaningful language
- Lack of opportunities for interaction and communication
- Lack of opportunities for comprehension and negotiation of meaning
- Lack of opportunities for exchanging previously unknown information.

This kind of set-up and distribution of roles in the language classroom *does not* lead to language acquisition and can only lead to the development of some kind of mechanical language-like behaviour.

What is the role of the instructor and the language learner?

In traditional instruction, the role of the language instructor is that of an authoritative transmitter of knowledge. The teacher possesses the knowl-edge about the language and he/she is willing to transfer that knowledge to the language learners. L2 learners play the role of note-takers. The following example is a typical one where the roles of language instructor and language learner are traditional:

1   Students are given ten minutes to complete individually a worksheet containing a multiple choice activity (filling the blanks with the correct grammatical element).
2   At the end of ten minutes, students are instructed to work in groups of three and come to an agreement on the correct answers.
3   After seven minutes the teacher calls for the class's attention and begins going over the correct answers one by one. The teacher reads each sentence to the class and calls on students to respond. The student provides the correct element to complete the sentence.
4   The teacher offers a lengthy explanation of particular grammatical elements both in the case when the student gives a correct or incorrect answer.

All actions and interactions and explanations in the above example are dictated by the language instructor (expert transmitter of knowledge). The learner's role is passive and is mainly to receive knowledge. The language instructor assumes full responsibility for all that goes on in the classroom. He or she supplies clear explanations about the language. L2 learners are not exposed to opportunities for interaction, interpretation, negotiation of meaning and overall communication during this practice. *It does not provide* opportunities for learners to use language in a meaningful and communicative way involving the exchange of messages. The role of the learner is to repeat and produce language accurately. Production of language is very restricted. In most cases, learners don't need to know what they are saying only that it is accurate. Teachers make use of drills and open-ended questions.

Imitation and repetition *do not play* a role in acquisition.

When we adopt an interactive language task, both language instructors and language learners play out more effective roles in the language classroom. In a more interactive and communicative classroom, language instructors play a different role. They develop language tasks so that language learners become more active/responsible for their own learning. In interactive communicative language tasks, language instructors possess the information and they are willing to supply the information but only if language learners take a more proactive role and gather the information themselves. The language learners task is not simply to listen and respond but to signal if and where comprehension has not taken place. Language instructors are the architects as they need to plan the different parts of a language task to ensure L2 learners are exposed to meaningful input and have opportunities for expression, interpretation and negotiation of meaning by interacting with their peers. L2 learners become the co-builders as they need to take responsibility and work through the different layers of the task in order to complete it.

In adopting a new role for the instructor and the learner we aim to develop a new approach to our lesson goals. In traditional instruction, lesson goals are often reduced to completing a chapter in a book or covering a particular form, set of vocabulary or a grammatical structure. When the language instructor plays the architect role, the lesson goals must be built by constructing a task which encompasses all the vocabulary, grammar, and language functions that need to be covered. An interactive task becomes our approach lesson objective.

This task will help us to identify the following:

- What type of vocabulary is necessary for students to complete the task?
- Which parts of grammar do students need to complete the task?
- What language functions would they need to complete the task?
- What content (information about a given topic) should be included?

Interactive tasks can be effectively used to structure our teaching in order to accomplish lesson goals (grammar, vocabulary, language functions). Language instructors must remember that language learning requires 'good input'. Therefore, L2 learners should be exposed to comprehensible and message-oriented input. Tasks are structured in a way that L2 learners can move from input practice to output practice. L2 learners should always have the opportunities to link lexical units or grammatical forms with their meanings before they are asked to produce them.

What are the main points?

The role of the instructor and the language learner has changed over the years as the centre of attention is now the learner and the internal mechanisms and processes involved in the acquisition of the second language.

- In traditional instruction, the role of the language instructor is that of an authoritative transmitter of knowledge. The instructor possesses the knowledge about the language and she/he is willing to transfer that knowledge to the language learners. L2 learners play the role of note-takers. This type of practice does not provide opportunities for L2 learners to use language in a meaningful way involving a real exchange of messages. L2 learners' role is reduced to that of a 'parrot' – simply repeating and producing language accurately. Production of language is very restricted and, in most cases, L2 learners don't need to know what they are saying.
- In a more interactive classroom, language instructors play the role of an architect. They plan and develop language tasks so that L2 learners become more actively responsible for their own learning. They become co-builders and are responsible for the completion of the language tasks. Language instructors also possess the information and are willing to supply the information but only if L2 learners play a more proactive role and gather the information themselves.
- Interactive language tasks promote acquisition and provide a purpose for language use. A task approach should be used to archive a specific lesson objective. Language instructors can build their lesson objectives using an information exchange task approach constructed in a way that encompasses (using sub-tasks) all the vocabulary, grammar, and language functions that need to be covered by L2 learners in the lesson.

What else can we read?

Ellis, R. (2003) *Task-based Language Learning and Teaching*. Oxford: Oxford University Press.

Lee, J. (2000) *Tasks and Communicating in Language Classrooms*. New York: McGraw-Hill.

Lee, J. and VanPatten, B. (2003) *Making Communicative Language Teaching Happen*. New York: McGraw-Hill.

Long, M. (2015) *Second Language Acquisition and Task-based Language Teaching*. Malden, MA: Wiley-Blackwell.

Nunan, D. (2004) *Task-based Language Teaching*. Cambridge, UK: Cambridge University Press

Savignon, S (2005) *Communicative Competence. Theory and Classroom Practice*. New York: McGraw-Hill.

VanPatten, B. (2003) *From Input to Output*. NJ: McGraw-Hill.

Willis, D. and Willis, J. (2007) *Doing Task-based Teaching*. Oxford: Oxford University Press.

18 Working Memory

Can we take a minute to think about this?

Working memory is a space within the mind that a person uses for online processing and storing information temporarily before it is either forgotten or stored in long-term memory. It plays a role in all forms of complex thinking, such as reasoning, problem solving, and language comprehension.

What is the nature and role of working memory?

Memory is the ability to encode, store and retrieve information. Three types of memory have been identified: (i) sensory memory; (ii) working memory; (iii) long-term memory.

(i)   Sensory memory is responsible for receiving the information through different modalities. This information is subsequently processed and only a small proportion of the information enters working memory.

(ii) Short-term (working) memory receives input from the sensory system and then transfers information to long-term memory capable of storing information for a longer period of time. Working memory consists of a limited capacity store and is supported by two systems: the phonological loop which is responsible for processing auditory information; and the visual-spatial sketchpad, which is responsible for processing visual information.

(iii) Long-term memory refers to a system for storing information, which can be retrieved at a later stage. The storage capacity is very difficult to quantify. It appears that items in long-term memory might be stocked in associative networks of form meaning mappings.

In all the memory models a central feature remains the purpose, capability and function of working memory. Working memory refers to the processing space in the mind/brain when a person holds and computes information. There are multiple theories and models of working memory, but what they all have in common is the idea that working memory has a limited capacity. That is, a person can only process and store in working memory a limited amount of information before it must be disposed of so that the person can continue processing new incoming information.

A range of empirical studies within a cognitive and psycholinguistic account of language acquisition have been conducted to investigate the role of working memory in second language acquisition. Overall these studies have provided empirical support for the view that working memory plays a direct role in the acquisition of an L2 under certain conditions of exposure: processing capacity; input; and task demands.

Information processing theory was applied to the input processing theoretical framework in the early 1980s–1990s. Research conducted during this period focused on the various factors and processes responsible for how L2 learners process input and, more importantly, what part of that input becomes intake. From an information processing perspective it was assumed that individuals have a limited capacity for attention and processing information.

Over the past few years, researchers and theorists have examined the role of attention and information processing in second language acquisition with the intention of shedding some light on how and when L2 learners focus their attention and select information. On the one hand, they argue that second language acquisition is driven by what L2 learners pay attention to and notice in the input. On the other hand, other scholars maintain that attention is only one factor responsible for the acquisition of an L2. Attention can be defined as a cognitive process used by learners to selectively concentrate on one thing while ignoring other things.

Many theorists have argued that L2 learners have limited capacity for processing information. This means that learners must select the incoming stimuli from several stimuli, otherwise activities that draw upon this limited supply of attention will interfere with each other. One of the questions addressed by research is to establish what and how language learners initially select and process in the input. Detection refers to the process responsible for selecting, engaging a specific piece of information and registering this information in memory. Detection, and not selection and noticing, is the key element for the derivation of intake from the L2 input.

From an input processing perspective, input gets 'hanged' when L2 learners attend to too many stimuli, and therefore L2 learners filter the information utilising internal strategies to cope with the amount of information they receive. The input processing capacity of L2 learners is limited and their internal processors might not detect all the linguistic data available. One of the key questions is: what causes certain stimuli in the input to be detected and not others? When learners process input, they filter the input, which is reduced and modified into a new entity called 'intake'. Only part of the input L2 learners receive is processed and becomes intake. This is mainly due to processing limitations, as our working memory does not have enough capacity to do much more than process content words. Input processing consists of two sub-processes: making form-meaning connections; and parsing. VanPatten has identified a series of processing strategies/principles used by L2 learners when they process and filter linguistic data at input level. These strategies/principles allow learners to selectively attend to incoming stimuli without being overloaded with information. The two main principles of input processing theory are:

1   The Primacy of Meaning Principle. Learners process input for meaning before they process it for form.
2   The First Noun Principle. Learners tend to process the first noun or pronoun they encounter in a sentence as the subject/agent.

According to the first principle, during input processing, L2 learners initially direct their attention towards the detection of content words to understand the main meaning of an utterance. Learners tend to focus their attention on content words in order to understand the message of the input they are exposed to. In doing so, they do not process the grammatical form, and consequently fail to make form-meaning connections.

According to the second principle, L2 learners tend to process the first noun or pronoun they encounter in a sentence as the subject or agent. This processing strategy leads L2 learners to misinterpret the meaning of an utterance and causes a delay in acquisition.

The capacity of attention refers to the degree of attention allocated to the processing of information at any one time. Attention has a limited capacity as the sensory system of the brain is presented with a large amount of stimuli at any one time, and due to working memory constraints it is impossible to process them all. Both the number of stimuli and the amount of attention paid to each of them is therefore restricted.

The third concept related to the construct of attention refers to the learners' effort in processing information. It is assumed that sustained attention to a stimuli is essential for carrying out a task. The degree of effortful attention to a task depends on the capacity demands of the task. If the task is high in capacity demands then more effortful attention is needed for the performance, and processing might deteriorate. Less attention-demanding tasks allow L2 learners to process more information and conduct a secondary task.

What are the main points?

- Working memory is a psychological construct that refers to the processing space in the mind/brain when a person computes information.
- Working memory is an essential element (although it has a limited capacity in humans) in developing our ability to process linguistic data. It does play a central role in language processing (its ability to process symbols, store capacity and integrate information) in both comprehension and production of language.

What else can we read?

Baddeley, A.D. (2000) The episodic buffer: A new component of working memory? *Trends in Cognitive Science*, 4: 417–23. https://doi.org/10.1016/s1364-6613(00)01538-2

Robinson, P. (2003) Attention and memory during SLA. In Doughty, C. and Long, M.H. (eds), *The Handbook of Second Language Acquisition* (631–79). Oxford: Blackwell.

Stevick, E.W. (1996) *Memory, Meaning and Method: A View of Language Teaching*. Boston, MA: Cengage Learning.

Epilogue

Our definitions and reflections in each of the entries in this pocket guide are the fruit of theoretical views and empirical findings in second language acquisition. In this pocket guide, the entries reflect some of the issues and terms debated in the field of language learning and teaching. Some points have emerged in reviewing these terms/issues: (i) current beliefs from language instructors and L2 learners very often do not match what we know about how languages are learned and should be taught; (ii) instructional efforts have often limited effects on language learning. The question is: how can we provide opportunities for acquisition to happen? In this epilogue we briefly discuss the role that second language acquisition theory and research might and should play in creating such opportunities.

Second language acquisition is a vibrant and busy field of enquiry. It has evolved over the years to include research areas such as linguistics, psychology, education and neuroscience. The study of second language acquisition is the study of how second language learners create a new language system and how they make use of that system during comprehension and speech production. Over the years, scholars in this field have developed a series of theories, theoretical views and hypotheses about the way language learners develop a new language system that is not their first language. Fundamental questions raised in the field have been: Are L1 and L2 acquisition fundamentally the same or fundamentally different? What does development look like? What are the roles of input and output? What constraints are there on acquisition? We need to have a clear understanding of the nature and role of language. Research in second language learning/acquisition has provided us with some answers to our key questions so that we are now in a better position to develop our understanding of how a language is learned.

Here is what we know about second language acquisition:

(a) Language as mental representation is different from developing a language skill. Language is a complex, abstract and implicit system.

(b) Second language acquisition is primarily a matter of developing implicit knowledge.

(c) Input is the key ingredient in the process of acquisition.

(d) L2 learners require extensive input exposure to build their internal language systems apart from some universals exceptions.

(e) Input needs to be easily comprehended and message-oriented to be processed effectively by L2 learners. Input plays an essential role in second language acquisition. Most theories of second language acquisition assign a key role to input. If language learners are not exposed to comprehensible and meaningful input, they will not process language effectively. Comprehensible input is language input that is easy to process. Good input for acquisition is not explanation about grammar, or the presentation of vocabulary followed by mechanical practice. Good input is about creating opportunities for language learners to hear or read language that they need to process for meaning in order to make appropriate form–meaning mappings.

(f) L2 learners focus primarily on meaning when they process elements of the new language. Acquisition requires learners to make appropriate and efficient form–function connections (the relation between a particular form and its meaning/s).

(g) Interaction with other speakers, negotiation of meaning and corrective feedback may facilitate acquisition.

(h) L2 learners process linguistic features following a natural order and a specific sequence (i.e. they master different grammatical structures in a relatively fixed and universal order and they pass through a sequence of stages to master grammatical structure).

(i) Instruction might have a facilitative role through input manipulation and pedagogical interventions. The traditional practice in teaching grammar is that:

   (a) Language teachers instruct L2 learners about some specific grammatical forms (explicit information often using paradigms).

   (b) L2 learners practise the target forms through mechanical practice.

   (c) At the end language teachers assess them using paper–pencil tests.

There are *two problems* with this type instruction aiming at developing explicit knowledge:

(1) It does not correspond to the way language develops in our mind/brain.
(2) It does not correspond to the way L2 learners process information.

In the last 40 years a good deal has been learned about the effects of formal instruction in relation to what we already know about second language acquisition more generally. Language instruction cannot ignore the findings of second language research and must be informed by it. For example, if we know that particular linguistic structures are acquired in a particular order over time, what is the purpose of instruction on those same structures? If an instructor believes he or she can get learners to learn something early that is normally acquired later in acquisition, is that instructor making the best use of his or her time? When researchers in ISLA choose to examine the effects of formal instruction, how do they select the linguistic features and why do they select the ones they do? These are important questions and it is SLA research that can help to inform instructors and researchers about the choices they make.

Although researchers will continue to investigate second language acquisition from different perspectives in an attempt to develop a more complete picture of how languages are learned, the field needs to re-focus on the key issues and questions, adopting more sophisticated methodological tools to fully understand how the mind/brain process a second language, and creating a new system. Our perspective is that even though a significant gap exists between research on second language acquisition and teacher expectations, there is enough of second language acquisition research in existence that is useful for general teacher edification.

Many questions remain unanswered. Others are in need of more complete answers. The field has increased in size and scope, yet it is still sufficiently focused on questions of learning and teaching for many voices and perspectives to be acknowledged. The richness and complexity of SLA as a learning process and a field of study suggest that there are many perspectives to apply and many more applications to be found. SLA research must continue to investigate the nature of language itself by researching the following:

(i) how language is represented in the mind/brain (theoretical linguistics);

(ii) how language is produced and comprehended (applied language research, psycholinguistics);

(iii) how universality/constraints imposed by the human mind/brain along with the effects of bilingualism affect acquisition (first, second and third language acquisition); and

(iv) how languages can be replicated, modelled, and evaluated through technology.

Future research in SLA should make use of new technology (e.g. EEG, eye tracking, computational modelling and assessment, etc.) to track what happens within language learners' brains in real teaching/acquisition contexts. While behavioural studies can track only the automatisation of (second) language knowledge, multidisciplinary and high-tech research could track the internalisation of this knowledge. This research would significantly widen the horizons of language acquisition research and will have a major impact on the speed with which we learn languages (people skills), the way languages are taught (teacher skills), and the way languages are taught and assessed (educational policies, policy makers).

To conclude, if we were to make some suggestions for an acquisition-driven approach to language teaching, our suggestions would be:

1   The more we expose L2 learners to comprehensible and meaningful input the better!

2   The more we modify and expose L2 learners to language input linguistically and non-linguistically (use of pictures, cartoons, drawings, etc.) the better!

3   The more we engage L2 learners with opportunities for interaction and negotiation of meaning the better!

4   The more we engage with L2 learners with opportunities to produce the language for the purpose of expressing some kind of meaning the better!

5   The more we provide focus on form of the kind that it is meaning-based and tied to input and communication the better!

6   The more we engage L2 learners with tasks when they are taking a more active role in interpreting and eventually producing the target language the better!

7 The more we expose L2 learners to meaningful activities in which they need to exchange previously unknown information the better!

8 The more we use genuine questions as opposed to display questions the better!

9 The more we give L2 learners opportunities to self-repair their errors in the input they are exposed to the better!

10 The more we expose L2 learners to multiple instances of frequent words in a meaningful context the better!

Bibliography

Asher, J. (1977) *Learning Another Language Through Actions: The Complete Teacher's Guide Book*. Los Gatos, CA: Sky Oaks Productions.

Bachman, L. and Palmer, A. (1996) *Language Testing in Practice*. Oxford: Oxford University Press.

Baddeley, A. D. (2000) The episodic buffer: A new component of working memory? *Trends in Cognitive Science*, 4: 417–23. https://doi.org/10.1016/S1364-6613(00)01538-2

Barcroft, J. (2018) *Vocabulary in Language Teaching*. New York: Routledge.

Benati, A. (2013) *Key Issues in Second Language Teaching*. London: Equinox.

Benati, A. (2014) Second Language Acquisition. In Fäcke, C. (ed.), *Language Acquisition* (179–97). New York: Mouton de Gruyter.

Benati, A. (2017) Classroom-oriented research: Processing Instruction (findings and implications). *Language Teaching*, 52: 343–59. https://doi.org/10.1017/s0261444817000386

Benati, A. (2020) *Key Questions in Language Teaching*. Cambridge: Cambridge University Press.

Benati, A. (2021) *Focus on Form*. Cambridge: Cambridge University Press.

Benati, A. and Lee, J. (2008) *Grammar Acquisition and Processing Instruction*. Clevedon: Multilingual Matters.

Benati, A. and Schwieter, J. (2019) Pedagogical interventions to L2 grammar instruction. In Schwieter, J. and Benati, A. (eds), *The Cambridge Handbook of Language Learning* (475–99). Cambridge: Cambridge University Press.

Birdsong, D. (1999) *Second Language Acquisition and the Critical Period Hypothesis*. Mahwah, NJ: Lawrence Erlbaum Associates.

Birdsong, D. (2005) Interpreting age effects in second language acquisition. In Kroll, J. and de Groot, A.M.B. (eds), *Handbook of Bilingualism: Psycholinguistic Approaches* (109–27). Oxford: Blackwell.

Birdsong, D. and Paik, J. (2008) Second language acquisition and ultimate attainment. In Spolsky, B. and Hult, F. (eds), *Handbook of Educational Linguistics* (424–36). Oxford: Blackwell.

Bley-Vroman, R. (2009) The evolving context of the Fundamental Difference Hypothesis. *Studies in Second Language Acquisition*, 31: 175–98. https://doi.org/10.1017/s0272263109090275

Brown, S. (2011) *Listening Myths*. University of Michigan Press.

Brown, H.D. and Abeywickrama, P. (2010) *Language Assessment: Principles and Classroom Practices*. White Plains, NY: Pearson Education.

Buck, G. (2001) *Assessing Listening*. Cambridge: Cambridge University Press.

Bygate, M (1987) *Speaking*. Oxford: Oxford University Press.

Cho, Y. (2003) Assessing writing: Are we bound by only one method? *Assessing Writing*, 8: 165–91. https://doi.org/10.1016/s1075-2935(03)00018-7

Chomsky, N. (1965) *Aspects of the Theory of Syntax*. Cambridge, MA: MIT Press.

Clahsen, H. and Felser, C. (2006) How native-like is non-native language processing? *Trends in Cognitive Sciences*, 10: 564–70. https://doi.org/10.1016/j.tics.2006.10.002

Dave, W. and Willis, J. (2007) *Doing Task-Based Teaching*. Oxford, UK: Oxford University Press.

De Angelis, G. (2007) *Third or Additional Language Acquisition*. Clevedon: Multilingual Matters.

DeKeyser, R.M. (2007) *Practice in a Second Language. Perspectives from Applied Linguistics and Cognitive Psychology*. Cambridge: Cambridge University Press.

DeKeyser, R. (2015) Skill Acquisition Theory. In VanPatten, B. and Williams J. (eds), *Theories in Second Language Acquisition* (94–112). New York: Routledge.

Doughty C. and Williams, J. (1998) *Focus on Form in Classroom Second Language Acquisition*. New York: Cambridge University Press.

Dornyei, Z. (2001) *Motivational Strategies in the Language Classroom*. Cambridge: Cambridge University Press.

Dornyei, Z. (2001) *Teaching and Researching Motivation*. Harlow: Longman.

Dornyei, Z. (2005) *The Psychology of the Language Learner: Individual Differences in Second Language Acquisition*. Mahwah, NJ: Lawrence Erlbaum Associates.

Ellis, R. (2003) *Task-Based Language Learning and Teaching.* Oxford: Oxford University Press.

Ellis, R. (2016) Focus on form: A critical review. *Language Teaching Research*, 20: 405–28. https://doi.org/10.1177/1362168816628627

Field, J. (2008) *Listening in the Language Classroom.* Cambridge: Cambridge University Press.

Fulcher, G. (2013) *Practical Language Testing*. London: Routledge.

Gass, S. (2003) Input and Interaction. In Doughty, C. and Long, M. (eds), *The Handbook of Second Language Acquisition* (224–55). Oxford: Blackwell.

Gass, S. and Selinker, L. (2008) *Second Language Acquisition: An Introductory Course*. New York: Routledge.

Gass, S.M., Behney, J. and Plonsky, L. (2013) *Second Language Acquisition: An Introductory Course*. New York: Routledge.

Gass, S.M. and Mackey, A. (2015) Input, interaction and output in second language acquisition. In VanPatten, B. and Williams, J. (eds), *Theories in Second Language Acquisition* (180–206). New York: Routledge.

Grabe, W. (2009) *Reading in a Second Language: Moving from Theory to Practice*. New York: Cambridge University Press.

Green, A. (2013) *Exploring Language Assessment and Testing: Language in Action*. London: Routledge.

Hatch, E.M. (1983) Simplified input and second language acquisition. In Andersen, R.W. (ed.), *Pidginization and Creolization as Language Acquisition* (64–86). Cambridge, MA: Newbury House.

Herschensohn, J. and Young-Scholten, M. (2013) *The Cambridge Handbook of Second Language Acquisition*. Cambridge: Cambridge University Press.

Hinkel, E. (2005) (ed.) *Handbook of Research in Second Language Teaching and Learning*. Mahwah, NJ: Lawrence Erlbaum Associates.

Hummel K.M. (2014) *Introducing Second Language Acquisition. Perspectives and Practices*. West Sussex, UK: John Wiley & Sons, Inc.

Keating, G. (2018) *Second Language Acquisition. The Basics*. New York: Routledge

Krashen, S.D. (1982) *Principles and Practice in Second Language Acquisition*. New York: Pergamon Press.

Krashen, S. and Terrell, T. (1983) *The Natural Approach: Language Acquisition in the Classroom*. Hayward, CA: Alemany Press.

Larsen-Freeman, D. (2000) *Techniques and Principles in Language Teaching*. Oxford: Oxford University Press.

Lee, J. (2000) *Tasks and Communicating in Language Classrooms*. New York: McGraw-Hill.

Lee, J. and VanPatten, B. (2003) *Making Communicative Classroom Happens*. New York: McGraw-Hill.

Lichtman, K. and VanPatten, B. (2021) Was Krashen right? Forty years later. *Foreign Language Annals*, 54(2): 283–305. https://doi.org/10.1111/flan.12552

Littlewood, W. (1981) *Communicative Language Teaching. An Introduction.* Cambridge: Oxford University Press.

Long, M. (1996) The role of the linguistic environment in second language acquisition. In Ritchie, W. and Bhatia, T. (eds), *Handbook of Second Language Acquisition* (413–68). San Diego: Academic Press.

Long, M. (2007) *Problems in SLA*. Mahwah, NJ: Lawrence Erlbaum Associates.

Long, M. (2015) *Second Language Acquisition and Task-Based Language Teaching*. Malden, MA: Wiley-Blackwell.

Long, M. (2018) A micro process-product study of CLIL lesson: linguistic modifications, content dilution and vocabulary knowledge. *Instructed Second Language Acquisition*, 2: 3–38. https://doi.org/10.1558/isla.33605

Long, M. and Doughty, C. (2009) *The Handbook of Language Teaching.* Oxford: Wiley-Blackwell.

Lyster, R. and Ranta, L. (1997) Corrective feedback and learner uptake: Negotiation of form in communicative classrooms. *Studies in Second Language Acquisition*, 19: 37–66. https://doi.org/10.1017/S0272263197001034

Morgan-Short, K. (2021) Considering the updated Input Hypothesis from a neurolinguistic perspective: A response to Lichtman and VanPatten. *Foreign Language Annals*, 54(2): 324–330. https://doi.org/10.1111/flan.12551

Muňoz, C. (2006) *Age and the Rate of Foreign Language Learning.* Clevedon: Multilingual Matters.

Nassaji, H. (2015) *The Interactional Feedback Dimension in Instructed Second Language Learning*. London: Bloomsbury.

Nassaji, H. and Fotos, S. (2011) *Teaching Grammar in Second Language Classrooms*. New York: Routledge.

Nation, I.S.P. (2001) *Learning Vocabulary in Another Language.* Cambridge: Cambridge University Press.

Nunan, D. (2004) *Task-Based Language Teaching.* Cambridge: Cambridge University Press.

Ortega, L. (2008) *Understanding Second Language Acquisition.* Oxford: Oxford University Press.

Pienemann, M. (1998) *Language Processing and L2 Development.* Amsterdam: John Benjamins.

Pienneman M. and Kessler, J.-U. (2011) *Studying Processability Theory.* Amsterdam: John Benjamins.

Pienemann, M. and Lenzing, A. (2015) Processability theory. In VanPatten, B. and Williams, J. (eds), *Theories in Second Language Acquisition* (159–79). New York: Routledge.

Polio, C. (2018) *Teaching Second Language Writing*. New York: Routledge.

Read, J. (2013) Second language vocabulary assessment. *Language Teaching*, 46: 41–52. https://doi.org/10.1017/s0261444812000377

Richards, J.C. (2012) *Tips for Teaching Listening*. London: Pearson.

Richards, J.C. and Rodgers, T. S. (2001) *Approaches and Methods in Language Teaching*. Cambridge: Cambridge University Press.

Robinson, P. (2003) Attention and Memory during SLA. In Doughty, C. and Long, M.H. (eds), *The Handbook of Second Language Acquisition* (631–79). Oxford: Blackwell.

Rost, M. (2002) *Teaching and Researching Listening. Applied Linguistics in Applied Linguistics in Action.* London: Longman.

Rost, M. and Wilson, J. (2013) *Active Listening*. London: Pearson.

Wilson, J.J. (2008) *How to Teach Listening*. Pearson Longman.

Savignon, S. (2005) *Communicative Competence. Theory and Classroom Practice*. New York: McGraw-Hill.

Schwieter, J.W. (2015) *The Cambridge Handbook of Bilingual Processing*. Cambridge: Cambridge University Press.

Schwieter, J. and Benati, A. (2019) *The Cambridge Handbook of Language Learning*. Cambridge: Cambridge University Press.

Sheen, Y. (2011) *Corrective Feedback, Individual Differences and Second Language Leaning*. New York: Springer.

Singleton, D. (2007) The critical period hypothesis. Some problems. *Interlinguistica*, 17: 48–56.

Stevick, E.W. (1996) *Memory, Meaning and Method: A View of Language Teaching*. Cencage Learning.

Swain, M. (1995) Three functions of output in second language learning. In Cook, G. and Seidlhofer, B. (eds), *Principles and Practice in Applied Linguistics* (125–44). Oxford: Oxford University Press.

Taylor, L. (2011) *Examining Speaking: Research and Practice in Assessing Second Language Speaking*. Cambridge: Cambridge University Press.

Ullman, M. (2001) The declarative/procedural model of lexicon and grammar. *Journal of Psycholinguistic Research*, 30: 37–69. https://doi.org/10.1023/A:1005204207369

VanPatten, B. (2003) *From Input to Output*. NJ: McGraw-Hill.

VanPatten, B. (2004) On the role(s) of input and output in making form-meaning connections. In VanPatten, B., Williams, J., Rott, S. and Overstreet, M. (eds), *Form-Meaning Connections in Second Language Acquisition* (29–47). Mahwah, NJ: Lawrence Erlbaum Associates.

VanPatten, B. (2010) Two faces of SLA: Mental representation and skill. *Journal of English Studies*, 10: 1–18. https://doi.org/10.6018/ijes/2010/1/113951

VanPatten, B. (2015) Foundations of processing. *International Review of Applied Linguistics*, 53: 91–109. https://doi.org/10.1558/isla.40640

VanPatten, B. (2015) Input processing in adult SLA. In VanPatten, B. and Williams, J. (eds), *Theories in Second Language Acquisition* (113–35). New York: Routledge.

VanPatten, B. (2016) Why explicit knowledge cannot turn into implicit knowledge. *Foreign Language Annals*, 49: 650–57. https://doi.org/10.1111/flan.12226

VanPatten, B. and Williams, J. (2007) *Theories in Second Language Acquisition*. Mahwah, NJ: Lawrence Erlbaum Associates.

VanPatten, B. and Benati, A. (2010) *Key Terms in Second Language Acquisition*. London: Continuum.

VanPatten, B. and Rothman, J. (2014) Against rules. In Benati, A., Laval, C. and Arche, M. (eds), *The Grammar Dimension in Instructed Second Language Learning* (15–35). London: Bloomsbury.

VanPatten, B. and Benati, A. (2015) *Key Terms in Second Language Acquisition*. London: Bloomsbury.

VanPatten, B., Smith, M. and Benati, A. (2020) Key *Questions in Second Language Acquisition*: *An Introduction*. Cambridge: Cambridge University Press.

Vetter, E. (2012) Multilingualism pedagogy: building bridges between languages. In Hüttner, J., Schiftner, B., Mehlmauer, B. and Reichl S. (eds), *Theory and Practice in* EFL *Teacher Education. Bridging the G*ap (228–46). Bristol: Multilingual Matters.

Williams, J. (2005) *Teaching Writing in Second and Foreign Language Classrooms*. NJ: McGraw-Hill.

Willis, D. and Willis, J. (2007) *Doing Task-Based Teaching*. Oxford: Oxford University Press.

Wilson, J.J. (2008) *How to Teach Listening*. Pearson Longman.

White, L. (2003) *Second Language Acquisition and Universal Grammar*. Cambridge: Cambridge University Press.

Wong, W. (2005) *Input Enhancement: From Theory and Research to the Classroom*. New York: McGraw-Hill.

Wong, W. and VanPatten, B. (2003) The evidence in IN: Drills are out. *Foreign Language Annals*, 36: 403–23. https://doi.org/10.1111/j.1944-9720.2003.tb02123.x

Wong, W. and Simard, D. (2018) *Focusing on Form in Language Instruction*. New York: Routledge.

Zhao, H.H. and Anderson, N.J. (2009) *Second Language Reading Research and Instruction: Crossing the Boundaries*. Ann Arbor, MI: University of Michigan Press.

CPSIA information can be obtained
at www.ICGtesting.com
Printed in the USA
BVHW060731090222
628134BV00008B/120